Gillian Tait

111 Places
in the Lothians and Falkirk
That You
Shouldn't Miss

emons:

Bibliographical information of the Deutsche Nationalbibliothek
The Deutsche Nationalbibliothek lists this publication in
the Deutsche Nationalbibliografie; detailed bibliographical data
are available on the internet at http://dnb.d-nb.de.

Layout: Eva Kraskes, based on a design
by Lübbeke | Naumann | Thoben
Maps: altancicek.design, www.altancicek.de
Basic cartographical information from Openstreetmap,
© OpenStreetMap-Mitwirkende, OdbL
Edited by: Ros Horton
Printing and binding: Grafisches Centrum Cuno, Calbe
Printed in Germany 2024
ISBN 978-3-7408-1569-1
First edition

Guidebooks for Locals & Experienced Travellers
Join us in uncovering new places around the world at
www.111places.com

Foreword

There are numerous guides extolling the sights of Edinburgh (including my own, the first that I wrote for the 111 Places series), but few that explore the manifold attractions of its surroundings. This book sets out to redress the balance, taking the reader across a broad arc of terrain encompassing the three old counties of the Lothians that flank the capital, and extending west to Falkirk, at the heart of the Central Lowlands. It's an exceptionally diverse area in every sense, teeming with an extraordinary variety of unique places of interest.

I've done my best not to resort to well-worn clichés in my descriptions of these places, avoiding overused terms like 'hidden treasure', 'tucked away' and so on. However, as the project reaches completion, I can't resist indulging myself in one platitude: this book has been quite a journey. In a literal sense, it has of course involved a huge amount of travel, by bus and train, on foot, occasionally by car and also, most enjoyably, by boat and barge. But it has also been a voyage of personal discovery, revealing many surprises in areas that I thought I knew well, and altering my perception of others that I hadn't previously explored. It was a truly memorable experience that has deepened my appreciation of this remarkable stretch of country, and of the countless people who have shaped its history and character.

All of these 111 places (as well as those described in the 111 accompanying tips) are within easy reach of Edinburgh, though of course you don't have to start from there. It's my hope that this volume will not only encourage visitors to Central Scotland to seek out lesser-known destinations outside our desperately overtouristed capital city, but also inspire residents of the districts covered within its pages to explore the wealth of fascinating sites and sights to be found just a little way beyond their own doorsteps.

Gillian Tait

111 Places

1__ The Submarine Wrecks
Incredible hulks abandoned on the strand

Aberlady Bay is a 582-hectare tract of unspoilt terrain, protected since 1952, when it became the UK's first Local Nature Reserve in recognition of the importance and diversity of its flora, fauna and geology. An underlying motive for this designation was, rather soberingly, to control the indiscriminate shooting of wildfowl in the area; new post-war legislation had advocated encouraging the British public in 'the peaceful contemplation of nature'.

The walkway by which you enter the reserve was immortalised by local author Nigel Tranter as 'the footbridge to enchantment'. It's a wonderfully exhilarating expanse of land, with big skies, stunning horizons and a remarkable variety of habitats – woodland, freshwater loch, grassland, salt marshes, dunes and finally a vast golden beach. Two thirds of the reserve is submerged at high tide, and it's only when the sea is a long way out that its most curious, man-made feature is visible: the skeletal hulks of two submarines, relics of World War II, stranded on the sands.

These wrecks have truly undergone a sea change, transformed into 'something rich and strange'. One of them might be a giant green locust in its death throes; the other recalls the nightmarish aliens of H. R. Giger. Their earlier history, as training models of the X-class midget submarine, is scarcely less astonishing. Carrying a cramped crew of four, and powered by a London bus engine, the 52-foot-long X-Craft played a key role in several daring operations. The most famous was in September 1943, when two craft succeeded in putting the German battleship *Tirpitz* out of action in a Norwegian fjord, an odds-defying mission recounted in the 1955 film *Above Us the Waves*, starring the ubiquitous John Mills. The Aberlady pair were moored here shortly after the war for use as targets in aerial bombing trials, and then abandoned – a sadly ignominious fate for vessels with such a heroic past.

Address Aberlady Bay Local Nature Reserve, Aberlady, EH32 0QB | Getting there
Bus 124 or X24 to Aberlady Nature Reserve (request stop). Cross the footbridge and follow
the footpath to the beach, turning left at the junction (about 1.5 miles); the submarines are a
0.75 mile walk to the west | **Hours** Only visible at low tide; check tide times carefully before
setting out (www.tideschart.com) | **Tip** Hidden in a wood on the other side of the A198 is
an arched tomb with an effigy of an unknown knight in armour, almost all that remains
of the 13th-century Luffness Friary. It can be reached from Aberlady village by following
Postman's Walk, a footpath leading west at the end of Smiddy Brae.

2 Waterston House

A passion for birds

Birdwatching – or birding, as dedicated enthusiasts prefer to call it – is an increasingly popular activity in the UK. There was a boom in interest during the Covid lockdowns, when thousands of people new to bird spotting were inspired by a media campaign to observe and record the species visible in their own backyards. It was a valuable demonstration that you don't need to travel to exotic locations to have your eyes opened to the wonder of the elemental creatures we casually refer to as our feathered friends.

Even if your previous experience is limited to watching blue tits squabbling on a garden feeder, you're sure to be inspired by a visit to the Scottish Ornithologists' Club headquarters, home to a welcoming resource centre, open to all, named in honour of conservation pioneer George Waterston. In a tranquil setting on the edge of Aberlady Bay Nature Reserve, it's surrounded by diverse habitats – a pond, wildflower meadows and an attractive garden – that encourage a wide variety of bird life; more than a hundred species have been recorded. The building itself was designed for minimal impact, constructed from untreated Scottish timber using traditional techniques, with insulation made from old car windscreens.

Inside you'll find not only the most comprehensive collection of ornithological books in Scotland, but a bright, airy gallery with changing exhibitions by artists who specialise in wildlife. One popular regular exhibitor is long-time East Lothian resident Darren Woodhead, an exceptional watercolourist whose exquisite bird studies are all created in the open air.

A range of optical equipment is on sale as well as books and gifts, and fun activities are available for children. Guided walks and events, led by experts, are organised throughout the year, and knowledgeable staff are always on hand to advise everyone from complete novice to obsessive twitcher.

Address Craigielaw, Aberlady, EH32 0PY, +44 (0)1875 871330, www.the-soc.org.uk | **Getting there** Bus 124 or X24 to Aberlady (the Pleasance) | **Hours** Wed–Sun 10am–5pm (4pm in winter) | **Tip** The East Lothian coast has several other excellent sites for birdwatching, including the Musselburgh Lagoons, where goosander can be observed at close range in the high summer, and Gosford Bay, the best place in Britain to view red-necked grebe.

3__ The Flag Heritage Centre

High may your proud standards gloriously wave!

Scotland's flag is a beauty – a classically simple design of a white diagonal cross, or saltire, on a blue background. It's both instantly memorable and stirringly evocative, with symbolism evoking St Andrew, who according to tradition was crucified on an X-shaped cross. Its true history is obscure, but this is amply made up for by an old legend linking it to Athelstaneford, the village that now claims the title 'Birthplace of Scotland's Flag'.

The tale tells of a nearby battle, fought in the Dark Ages when the Lothians were part of Northumbria. An army of Picts and Scots was about to face a much larger contingent of Anglo-Saxons when a diagonal cross of white clouds appeared against the azure sky. The Pictish king Óengus, taking this as a sign of heavenly support, vowed that if he won (which he did) he would make St Andrew his kingdom's patron saint.

First recounted by late medieval chroniclers, this origin story was given a new airing after the 20th-century rekindling of Scottish nationalism. Local historian and novelist Nigel Tranter championed Athelstaneford's claim to fame, and in 1965 a Saltire Memorial was erected in the kirkyard, along with a flagpole where the standard flies by day and night. Behind the church, a pennant flutters next to a beautifully restored doocot (pigeon house), the home since 1997 of the Flag Heritage Centre. It's a little gem, dating from 1583, with a splendid outlook over the supposed battle site. Inside, the traditional story is elaborated in an atmospheric audio-visual sequence, featuring a narrative taken from Tranter's novel *Kenneth*.

Like all the best legends, the story of the Saltire owes much to earlier myths, not least that of the Roman emperor Constantine and his vision of the Christian cross. But though it may not stand up to close historical scrutiny, it's a picturesque tale to enjoy in a picturesque spot.

Address Behind Parish Church, Main Street, Athelstaneford, EH39 5BE, www.scottishflagtrust.com | **Getting there** Train to Drem and a two-mile walk; bus 121 to Athelstaneford | **Hours** Apr–Oct & 30 Nov (St Andrew's Day) 9am–6pm | **Tip** Half a mile south-west of the village at EH39 4SA, look out for the unusual, low-lying ruin of Barnes Castle. Known locally as The Vaults, it was begun in the 1590s to an innovative symmetrical design, but abandoned after the owner's death with only the lower part complete.

4 The Waggonway Project
Connecting with the history of a vital commodity

Looking at Cockenzie today, it's hard to believe that this quiet coastal village was once a busy industrial centre, making the most of local resources – sea water and convenient seams of coal – for the manufacture of salt. Salt making became established along the Forth estuary in medieval times, and was given new impetus in the 17th century by improvements in mining technology.

In Cockenzie, the industry grew into such a lucrative business that in 1722 its harbour became the terminus of Scotland's first railway, built to connect the saltworks with coal mines at Tranent, and feed the fires that blazed day and night under vast pans of boiling brine. This was long before the age of steam locomotives – its rails were wooden, as were the waggons that travelled along them, drawn by horses or powered by gravity.

The story of this fascinating heritage is now being uncovered thanks to the dedicated volunteers of the 1722 Waggonway Project. In 2017 this multi-talented group of enthusiasts organised the first of a series of digs involving the local community, which soon revealed remains of both the salt pans and the original waggonway. The results of their ongoing work are on show in a museum packed with absorbing displays that cover every aspect of the historic industry. A sturdy replica waggon stands outside, often staffed by costumed members of the team who take on the roles of historic individuals; it's named in memory of James Paterson, who in 1762 became the first person to lose his life on a Scottish railway.

The group have also revived traditional saltmaking, with results that include the by-products of Oil of Salt (once a popular tonic, recommended for tired feet) and Pan Scratch, an alkaline powder similar to bath salts. Their latest plan is to build a working reconstruction of the waggonway itself, as the first phase of an ambitious living history project. Watch this space!

Address 1722 Waggonway Heritage Centre, West Harbour Road, Cockenzie, EH32 0HX, www.1722waggonway.co.uk | Getting there Bus 26 or X26 to Cockenzie (East Lorimer Place) | Hours Most Sats 10am–4pm; check website for details | Tip Nearby Cockenzie House is a late 17th-century mansion surrounded by gardens, probably built as a residence for the manager of the harbour and saltworks. In recent years it has found new life housing studios for artists and small businesses, and as a venue for regular public events including art exhibitions and fairs for crafts and collectibles.

5 Dirleton Castle

Medieval des-res in idyllic green setting

'This castle hath a pleasant seat': the well-known line from Shakespeare's 'Scottish play' fits Dirleton so neatly that it makes you wonder if the bard ever came here on a research trip. Dramatically perched on a craggy outcrop above a coastal plain, its desirable location is enhanced by a leisurely approach through glorious walled gardens, not to mention the old village that surrounds it, which is among the most attractive in southern Scotland.

The stronghold itself matches every child's picture of how a castle should look – a formidable cluster of round and square towers in honey-coloured stone, reached by a drawbridge spanning an encircling moat. Dating from the mid-13th century, it was home to three successive dynasties during its 400-year occupancy. Castle life was mostly peaceful, but it did see its fair share of violence and intrigue, including one hideous episode in 1649, when six local folk accused of witchcraft were imprisoned and interrogated here. Spine-tingling sights like the 'murder hole' above the entrance (for chucking rocks or hot liquids down on intruders), and stones grooved by guardsmen sharpening weapons, contrast with reminders of the nobility's leisured lifestyle, such as the exquisitely carved buffet in the banqueting hall, for showing off silverware.

Evidence has been found of a 16th-century 'pleasance', thought to have comprised a knot garden filled with herbs, as well as vegetable patches and orchards. A fine doocot (pigeon house) – another source of food – still stands almost intact. Some time after the castle was abandoned, the grounds were remodelled to complement the picturesque ruin, before a Victorian-era overhaul, when they were planted with elaborate geometric flower beds. The colourful north garden, reshaped in the 1920s in Arts and Crafts style, is overlooked by a charming turreted gazebo, now an interpretation centre exploring the history of both castle and garden.

Address Dirleton, EH39 5ER, +44 (0)1620 850465, www.historicenvironment.scot | Getting there Bus 122, 124 or X5 to Dirleton Castle | Hours Daily Apr–Sept 9.30am–12.30pm & 1.30–5.30pm, Oct–Mar 10am–12.30pm & 1.30–4pm | Tip Just off the village green and right opposite the castle, the Open Arms is a long-established, family-owned hotel with a high-quality restaurant offering lunch and dinner, and 12 comfortable rooms if you fancy a stay in delightful Dirleton.

6 Yellowcraig

Seaside bliss with a prospect of Feather Island

The pale golden strand of Yellowcraig is among the very finest of all the splendid beaches along East Lothian's 40-mile coastline. Part of its appeal comes from its naturally diverse coastal setting – the sandy cove and rocky outcrops are backed by a bracing sweep of dune grassland and scrub, which in turn gives way to mixed woodland, creating a whole array of habitats to explore, all of them rich in plant, animal and bird life. There's even a small hill on the seaward side of the wood – Yellow Craig itself, a fragment of an ancient volcano that makes a good viewpoint from which to survey your surroundings.

Out to sea is a scattering of small islands, one of them tantalisingly close to the shore. This is Fidra, 'a strange grey islet of two humps, made the more conspicuous by a piece of ruin', in the words of Robert Louis Stevenson. The author, who knew this coastline from boyhood holidays in North Berwick, is thought to have used his memories of its distinctive topography as the inspiration for *Treasure Island*, the hugely influential tale of buccaneers and buried gold that launched his career as a novelist.

Stevenson owed his maritime knowledge (and map-making skills) to his upbringing – he came from a family of lighthouse engineers, and trained in that profession himself for a time, albeit reluctantly. His cousin David designed Fidra's lighthouse, which dwarfs the scant remains of its medieval chapel and castle. Completed in 1885, it was automated in 1970, since when the island's only occupants have been its significant but fluctuating seabird population. Puffins in particular have suffered a decline, due to the spread of tree mallow (a plant once used by lighthouse keepers in lieu of toilet paper), but are recovering thanks to its regular removal by volunteers. This is especially satisfactory given that the name Fidra actually means 'feather island'.

Address Near Dirleton, EH39 5DS | Getting there Bus 122, 124 or X5 to Dirleton, then a 20-minute walk via Ware Road | Tip Family-friendly facilities in the woods include a pirate-themed adventure playpark and a network of nature trails, plus a novel environmental artwork, designed with input from local schools. For close-up views of the birds on Fidra, visit the Seabird Centre in North Berwick, which operates remote-control cameras on the island.

7 Belhaven Brewery

The eminently quaffable 'Burgundy of Scotland'

Beer may not be the drink most immediately associated with Scotland today, but it has a very much longer heritage than the upstart whisky. Evidence from Orkney shows that farming communities were malting and fermenting barley to make their own home brew at least 5,000 years ago. For millennia this remained a largely domestic activity, but in the Middle Ages the first great leap forward for Scottish beer came with the arrival of monks from continental religious orders, who introduced new production methods that formed the basis on which the modern brewing industry was built.

Around 1250, a plot of fertile, well-watered land at Belhaven, the 'beautiful harbour' of Dunbar, was granted to a group of brewing Benedictines based on the Isle of May and, remarkably, a brewery still stands on the same site to this day. The current incarnation can date its foundation to 1719, making it the oldest working brewery in Scotland by a long way.

Based in a picturesque cluster of historic buildings, and still using local spring water and barley from nearby fields, Belhaven Brewery is nonetheless a very modern operation these days, as you will learn if you take one of their informative and entertaining guided tours. With an award-winning range of craft beers, ales and stouts, they're proud to be part of a long tradition of excellence – 18th-century diarist and tippler James Boswell declared the small beer that he quaffed in Dunbar to be the best he'd ever tasted, and in 1827 Emperor Francis I of Austria made a point of choosing Belhaven's 80-shilling ale for his cellar, declaring it to be the 'Burgundy of Scotland'.

The tour ends at the in-house bar, named the Monks' Retreat in honour of those thirsty medieval brethren. A generous, tutored tasting session of a selection of brews is followed by a pint of your choice, personalised with your own photo uploaded on to the head.

Address Brewery Lane, Belhaven, Dunbar, EH42 1PE, +44 (0)845 6075325, www.belhaven.co.uk | Getting there Bus X7 to Belhaven | Hours Tours Mon–Sat 10.15am & 2.30pm | Tip Just over a mile east in Dunbar proper, Station Yard is an unusual find in these parts – a cosy artisan micropub in a historic building (a former coal house), with a sheltered outdoor seating area, and a log fire indoors for days when Dunny isn't so sunny. Right by the railway station (in case you hadn't guessed) it's run by Haddington-based Winton Brewery, and also serves other local beers, ciders and gins as well as a good range of whiskies.

8 Belhaven Bridge
You ain't goin' nowhere

Mention the word 'bridge' to any resident of the Lothians, and most thoughts will turn to the three marvels of engineering that carry rail and road traffic from Queensferry across the Forth to Fife. But for connoisseurs of curiosities there's another crossing 50 or so miles along the coast from these icons that is rapidly achieving a similar celebrity status, thanks to our photo-opportunity-obsessed era. It's a very much humbler affair, a simple little footbridge whose fame is based on the perverse illusion that, at times, it appears to have no purpose at all.

The Bridge to Nowhere, as it has been dubbed, stands just outside Dunbar in Belhaven Bay, a vast and magnificent expanse of sand backed by dunes and salt marsh. A sizeable stream, the Biel Water, discharges here into the North Sea, and the short footbridge across its shallow channel provides access to the golden strand for surfers, swimmers, dog exercisers and other beach users, as well as coastal walkers. The utilitarian metal structure is flanked on either side by concrete steps, plus walkways added to facilitate access across the rocky foreshore, and if you see this rather jumbled ensemble when the sea is out you'll wonder what all the fuss is about. It's only when the tide is high that the magic happens; the sand and lower structures are submerged as the water rises, leaving the bridge completely marooned in the sea.

This phenomenon occurs when the level gets above 16 feet, at the time of the twice-monthly spring tides, so be sure to check tide tables if you're planning a journey just to see it. (The use of 'spring' in this context has nothing to do with the season, by the way.) It's a surreal landmark that has inspired nearby Belhaven Brewery to create a beer in its honour: Bridge to Nowhere Pale Ale, which apparently makes your thirst disappear like the sands in the bay when the tide comes in.

Address Belhaven Beach, Shore Road, Belhaven, Dunbar, EH42 1NX | Getting there Train to Dunbar and a 1.5 mile walk; bus X7, 106, 120, 130 or 253 to Belhaven (Old Police Station) | Hours The bridge is marooned when the tide reaches a height of over 16 feet (5 metres); check online tide tables before travelling | Tip A mile along the coast is a cove that was once home to Dunbar Lido, the largest open-air swimming pool in Scotland. Created in the 1880s, it was later developed to comprise a pavilion, ballroom, promenade and boating pond. Swimming galas, beauty contests and the like were held regularly, and it was hugely popular for decades with both visitors and locals. Though it was demolished in 1984, some traces can still be seen in the bay, not far from the present-day Leisure Centre.

9_ Coast to Coast
Dancing with the Scottish waves

For at least 20 million enthusiasts around the world, surfing is much more than a mere pastime: many describe the first time they rode a wave as a truly life-changing moment. If you're one of those who have yet to experience this all-consuming sensory thrill, Belhaven Bay is an excellent place to do so. With a wide, flat, sandy beach and shallow water free from rocks, it's perfect for beginners – and it's also home to Scotland's leading surf school, Coast to Coast. Their team of instructors, led by the genial and highly experienced Sam Christopherson, offer relaxed but structured surfing tuition for all ages from 7 to well over 70, at levels from beginner to intermediate. You can also try stand-up paddleboarding, or a coasteering adventure (involving swimming, climbing and jumping off cliffs) around the stunning local shoreline – or even one of the school's four-day tours to the world-class surfing destinations of the north coast and the Western Isles.

Coast to Coast was established in 2004, and has since produced many champions and national team members, undoubtedly contributing to the huge recent growth in the popularity of the sport in Scotland – this country is now one of Europe's top surfing destinations, with autumn and winter, surprisingly, offering the best conditions.

Another surprise is that Scottish surfing history goes back well over half a century. Long before the age of purpose-made wetsuits, small groups of hardy pioneers began riding the North Sea waves around East Lothian and Aberdeen, at a time when most Scots saw it as a purely exotic pursuit, practised on sun-kissed Pacific shores to a Beach Boys soundtrack. So it was fitting that the purpose-built Belhaven Surf Centre, where Coast to Coast has been based since 2019, was opened by local legend Andy Bennetts, who first caught the waves in this bay back in September 1968.

Address Belhaven Surf Centre, 36 Back Road, Belhaven, EH42 1NX, +44 (0)7971 990361, www.c2csurfschool.com | Getting there Train to Dunbar and a 1.5 mile walk; bus X7, 106, 120, 130 or 253 to Belhaven (Old Police Station) | Hours Mar–Nov, daily 9am–5pm; sessions last two hours – book via website | Tip Less than two miles west is John Muir Alpacas, a recently established and already highly rated rural business offering alpaca trekking through the lovely coastal woodland of John Muir Country Park.

10 The Creel Loaders

Shouldering the silver darlings

Nestling in a hedge-fringed enclave near Dunbar Harbour is a delightfully offbeat tribute to the herring fisheries that were once the mainstay of the local economy. Hewn out of sandstone, it depicts a close-knit group of figures, including two sturdy men and a couple of frisky felines (a nod to Cat Row, the old name of the adjacent street), but the main subject is a quietly stoical woman, laden with a large basket. She's a fishwife, off to sell the catch of the day.

From the 17th to the 19th century, Dunbar was the foremost port in eastern Scotland for the trade in 'silver darlings', as they were called in the lyrical, superstition-rich language of fisher-folk. The coastal seas were then so densely filled with herring shoals as to merit the quip 'one third water and two thirds fish' from early guidebook author Daniel Defoe. The dangerous work of crewing the boats and bringing in the marine harvest was always a male preserve, but fishermen's wives and daughters played equally vital roles, working long hours in laborious tasks that began with baiting the lines and continued as soon as the catch was landed with gutting, cleaning and salt-curing. But selling the herring was the most arduous women's work of all – it meant travelling long distances on foot, carrying massive loads in creels on their backs. And Dunbar fishwives could cover the 27 miles to Edinburgh in just five hours.

It is to the unsung generations of these proud women that *The Creel Loaders* is dedicated. Unveiled in 2016, it was carved by Cockenzie stonemason turned sculptor Gardner Molloy, whose endearingly chunky figures celebrating local heritage are familiar around East Lothian. It's a riot of textures, relishing the weave of the clothing, the tactile wickerwork creel with smaller basket on top, and the carrying strap, worn (as is recorded in old photographs) around the fishwife's forehead.

Address Victoria Street (at junction with Castle Gate), Dunbar, EH42 1HR | Getting there
Train to Dunbar; bus X7, 120, 130 or 253 to Dunbar town centre | Tip The Dunbar Art
Trail takes in *The Creel Loaders* as well as 25 other monuments around the town, including
the 16-foot-high *DunBear* by Andy Scott (of *Kelpies* fame); see www.dunbararttrail.com
for details. Two other quirky statue groups by Gardner Molloy worth seeking out are
the monument to the Battle of Pinkie Cleugh, on the outskirts of Musselburgh, and the
Prestonpans Miners' Memorial.

11 Dunbar Battery
Cultural sea change for an old bastion of war

Lamer Island occupies a commanding site just off the rugged shores of Dunbar, between the town's two harbours. It has a chequered history of use by the local community that began in earnest in 1781, after two attacks by American ships during their War of Independence sparked the decision to construct a fort on the rocky outcrop, armed with a battery of 16 guns. The French Revolution and Napoleonic Wars created further threats, and a militia was formed to man the battery, but in the event they never fired a shot in anger. Later decades brought redevelopment of the harbour and a new lifting bridge linking the island to the mainland; the battery site then became home to a hospital for infectious diseases, requisitioned in World War I for military use, and it was even used for emergency housing before storm damage in 1936 made it uninhabitable.

A long period of neglect followed, until in 2015 Dunbar Harbour Trust initiated an inspired project to restore the ruinous landmark as a cultural resource, with an open-air performance space as its central feature. Completed two years later, the new Dunbar Battery incorporates artwork and interpretation as well as an arena, all sympathetically integrated into the historic structure. You can relax in the pebbled garden dotted with sea pinks and candytuft, wander among the striking *Sea Cubes* – sculptures in mirrored steel engraved with images of maritime creatures – and survey the far-reaching views from the breezy battlements, as you listen to the kittiwakes' haunting cries. The events programme includes the annual Black Agnes Festival, celebrating the heroine of the 1388 Siege of Dunbar Castle. But even if you're not lucky enough to catch a play or a concert, you must peruse the amphitheatre: its stepped timber seating is inscribed with the names of sea areas cherished by the countless landlubbers whose nightly ritual includes tuning in to the BBC's longest running radio programme, *The Shipping Forecast*.

Address Dunbar Harbour, Dunbar, EH42 1HS, www.dunbarbattery.org.uk | **Getting there** Train to Dunbar; bus X7, 106, 120, 130 or 253 to Dunbar town centre | **Hours** Always accessible, except in the case of extreme weather conditions. See website for events programme | **Tip** Dunbar Harbour is a great place to explore, with excellent information panels to help you appreciate its history and current use. As well as attractive fishing boats, there's a ruinous castle and sea cave to admire at a distance and wildlife to observe – kittiwakes, fulmars and other seabirds, plus grey seals (which seem to enjoy observing you back).

12 John Muir's Birthplace
'All the wild world is beautiful'

Dunbar's most illustrious son, John Muir, is a classic case of a prophet without honour in his own country. Long revered in his adoptive USA as the founder of the world's first national park system, Muir was a champion of wild nature – an environmental activist a century before the concept gained global momentum. But Scots were slow to heed the voice calling in the far-off wilderness, and until many decades after his death he went uncelebrated in the land of his birth.

Though he emigrated with his family just before his 11th birthday in 1849, Muir (who never lost his Scottish accent) always acknowledged the lasting influence on his life's work of his boyhood journeys of discovery, roaming the diverse and wondrous terrain around his home town. Dunbar's belated homage began in 1976, with the designation of eight miles of East Lothian coastline as the John Muir Country Park. Soon afterwards, negotiations began to acquire the much-altered 18th-century townhouse where he was born; the exterior was restored to reflect its original appearance, and finally in 1998 the John Muir Birthplace Trust was formed with the aim of converting the three-storey interior into a fitting monument to his life and legacy. This was realised in 2003 with the opening of an imaginatively conceived interpretive centre, which cleverly incorporates intriguing contemporary displays into the atmospheric shell of the historic building.

The ground floor evokes Muir's boyhood in Dunbar, while the upper storeys explore his travels in America and beyond, his beliefs and achievements, inviting visitors to ponder the relevance of his thinking to the urgent environmental issues of today. Muir was a prolific and eloquent author, and memorable use is made throughout the displays of inspirational quotations from his deeply felt writings, as well as vivid botanical sketches from his journals.

"What is the secret of the mysterious enjoyment felt here – the strange calm, the divine frenzy?"

"The clearest way into The Universe is through a forest wilderness."

"Everybody needs beauty as well as bread, places to play in and pray in, where Nature may heal and cheer and give strength to body and soul."

Address 126 High Street, Dunbar, EH42 1JJ, +44 (0)1368 865899, www.jmbt.org.uk | Getting there Train to Dunbar; bus X7, 106, 120, 140 or 253 to Dunbar town centre | Hours Apr–Sept, Mon–Sat 10am–5pm, Sun 1–5pm, Oct–Mar, Wed & Thu 10am–2.15pm, Fri–Sun 12.45–5pm | Tip Just across the street is the tall white clock tower of Dunbar Town House, a distinctive historic building that has been at the heart of civic life for more than 400 years. It has an atmospheric old Council Chamber where a series of notorious witch trials were once held, and the ground floor houses a small community museum with a programme of changing exhibitions on themes of local interest.

13 The Museum of Flight

Reaching for the sky

If you think that a collection of 50-plus old aeroplanes sounds strictly for aviation geeks, prepare to have your preconceptions shot down in flames. Sited on a historic airfield with a potently evocative atmosphere, Scotland's National Museum of Flight is winningly designed to engage the broadest possible audience. Its military, commercial and recreational aircraft (some of which can be boarded) are brought to vivid life in displays that focus not just on technological data, but on the filmed testimonies of individuals who were intimately connected with them – designers, engineers, pilots, crew and passengers. These are complemented by a variety of unique artefacts with their own stories to tell, and a choice of absorbing interactives for all ages where you can explore the principles of flight. Or perhaps try your hand at the virtual controls of Airship R.34, recalling the first ever aerial crossing from Britain to the USA, which began from this very airfield in 1919.

The museum opened in 1975, but first hit the headlines with its acquisition in 2004 of what's fondly known as Scotland's Concorde, the elegant supersonic airliner that once flew champagne-quaffing jet-setters across the pond so fast that its tagline was 'Arrive before you leave'. One particularly eye-catching item in the accompanying exhibition is the Senior Test Engineer's air-ventilated suit, whose bizarre styling could have come from the mind of Jules Verne.

A more chilling milestone in the perennial quest for high speed is the tiny Messerschmitt Komet, a revolutionary rocket-powered German fighter plane of World War II that could reach 600mph. The model now at East Fortune was flown in June 1945 by Scotsman Captain Eric 'Winkle' Brown, one of the world's greatest ever aviators, who recalled the experience in an interview at the museum shortly before his death at the age of 96.

Address East Fortune Airfield, East Fortune, EH39 5LF, +44 (0)300 1236789, www.nms.ac.uk/national-museum-of-flight | Getting there Bus 121 from North Berwick or Haddington to museum entrance | Hours Apr–Oct daily 10am–5pm, Nov–Mar, Sat & Sun 10am–4pm; advance booking recommended | Tip Nearby Fenton Barns is a retail and leisure development based on the site of a World War I aerodrome that was re-established shortly before World War II; a few strikingly Art Deco-styled buildings survive. It's home to a deservedly popular farm shop and café.

14__Preston Mill

Enchanting relic of the old daily grind

Among all the properties cared for by the National Trust for Scotland, there is one site with an appeal that is uniquely beguiling: not a castle, garden or stately home, but the curious old watermill that nestles quietly by the River Tyne just outside East Linton. Such is the fairy-tale charm of Preston Mill that it would be easy to disregard its original workaday, unromantic function if it weren't for the illuminating guided tours and displays, and the wealth of insights they give into the people and processes involved in the historic industry of grinding grain. Though the mill was last used commercially in 1959, for producing oatmeal – always the Scottish staple – the waterwheel is still operational, and the internal mechanisms can be observed as they go through their mesmerising cycle.

There were once grain mills near every village and hamlet in East Lothian – almost 100 existed in the 17th century, including Preston's. All were the property of landowners, leased at a substantial rent to millers, whose income came from payments in kind recouped from the tenant farmers who were compelled to have their grain ground there. Mercifully, this feudal system fell into decline in the 18th century, thanks to huge improvements in both agriculture and milling technology, but the life of the miller was still based on a gruelling routine of demanding skilled labour.

The kiln was where the crucial and tricky task of drying the grain took place, and this is the building at Preston that lends the complex its quirky character. With stonework swelled by *ad hoc* additions and grown-on buttressing, a conical roof swathed in a cascade of wavy pantiles and a wind vane carved with a hand outstretched in friendship, it has an irresistibly picturesque appearance, which was celebrated by painters long before the mill became a backdrop for film and TV. The most notable was Robert Noble, who moved to the village in the 1880s and later became first president of the Scottish Society of Artists.

Address Preston Road, East Linton, EH40 3DS, +44 (0)1620 860426, www.nts.org.uk |
Getting there Train to East Linton and a 15-minute walk; bus 120 to East Linton (The
Dean) or X7 to Bridgend Hotel and a 15-minute walk | **Hours** Mar–Oct, Thu–Mon
10.30am–3.30pm; guided tours on the hour, booking essential | **Tip** There are several lovely
walks in the near vicinity. A short, circular stroll from the mill takes you to Phantassie
Doocot, an unusual 16th-century pigeon house, and back along the riverbank, or you could
head to Smeaton Lake Woods, where there's a plant nursery and tearoom.

15_ Traprain Law

Ancient legend, buried treasure and cute ponies

Though classified by mountaineers as a mere hump (or 'Hundred and Upwards Metre Prominence'), the hog-backed crag of Traprain Law is a proud feature of the gentle East Lothian skyline. Formerly known as Dunpender, it stands 724 feet above sea level, dominating the expanse of open farmland east of Haddington. Today, its windswept heights are deserted save for a sturdy herd of Exmoor ponies, introduced to graze the species-rich natural grassland. But this rugged summit was once the site of a prosperous fortified town, home to countless generations from the late Bronze Age until medieval times. At its maximum extent it covered 40 acres, and traces of massive ramparts dating from the 1st century A.D. are still visible on many parts of the hill.

Archaeologists believe that this was the capital of the Votadini, the powerful rulers of south-east Scotland at the time of the Roman invasion, who apparently negotiated a treaty that allowed them to co-exist peacefully with the enemy. It was during an excavation in 1919 that the summit yielded astounding evidence of this relationship – a huge buried hoard of Roman 'hacksilver', weighing over 53 pounds and dateable to the mid-5th century A.D., the dying days of Britannia. Consisting chiefly of exquisite tableware, cut into pieces and flattened, this was most probably a payment for services rendered, given to a native chief who would have had it melted down and recast as impressively chunky status-symbol jewellery.

Legends claim Traprain as the home of King Loth, the Dark-Age hero of Arthurian romance who gave his name to the Lothians. Less creditably, he is also known in Early Christian lore as a brutal father, who had his daughter Thenew thrown from the hilltop on discovering her pregnancy. She survived, and despite then being cast adrift in the Forth, later gave birth to a son, who grew up to become the missionary and founder of Glasgow, St Mungo.

Address Near East Linton, EH41 4PY; the Traprain Law Treasure is on permanent display in the Early Peoples gallery at the National Museum of Scotland, Chambers Street, Edinburgh, EH1 1JF | Getting there From East Linton, take turning off A199 that goes under the A1. Turn right at junction and continue for 1.2 miles until the right turn (signposted) which leads to the parking area and path to the summit | Tip The excellent Bostock Bakery in East Linton has an open-plan café where you can watch the bakers at work as you enjoy lunch or a snack, featuring their signature sourdough bread and mouthwatering pâtisserie.

16 — Chippendale School of Furniture

Creating heirlooms for the future

At a time when many traditional craft skills seem doomed to extinction, it's a joy to discover that the fine art of cabinetmaking is not only alive but flourishing in a corner of rural East Lothian. Scotland's only independent furniture school, named in homage to the venerable Thomas Chippendale, occupies a handsome converted country manor in the rolling landscape just north of Gifford. Founded in 1985 by Anselm Fraser, whose son Tom took over as principal in 2019, the school was originally a small-scale enterprise specialising in furniture restoration. It grew gradually over the years into the centre of woodworking excellence that it is today, a melting pot of creativity rooted in a firm basis of hands-on training at the workbench. Students come from all over the world to learn and develop their skills under the guidance of its team of expert tutors; some have decided on a more rewarding career path after years of rat-race stress, others are seeking to turn a cherished hobby into a profession.

The flagship course offers an intensive and thorough grounding in traditional cabinetmaking, machine working and contemporary design, along with the skills necessary to set up in business. Its culmination is the graduate exhibition and sale of work, an annual showcase that attracts a steady stream of admiring visitors and potential customers. Students are only too happy to discuss their designs, and there's usually a friendly workshop dog or two padding about to add to the relaxed atmosphere.

If you're intrigued enough to try your hand at woodworking yourself, there's also a programme of shorter courses for beginners, covering specialist techniques such as woodturning, spoon carving, upholstery and antique restoration.

Address Myreside Grange, Cockles Brae, Gifford, EH41 4JA, +44 (0)1620 810680, www.chippendaleschool.com | Getting there On B 6369 1 mile north of Gifford; bus 123 from Haddington | Hours Graduate exhibition and sale of fine furniture held annually over three days in mid June; visiting slots bookable online | Tip Just west of Gifford village, The Bus Stop is a unique glamping site offering luxury and rustic accommodation in a collection of renovated static buses. It's based on a working farm with goats, sheep, chickens and alpacas, and each bus has its own private garden with panoramic views of the Lammermuir Hills.

17__Yester Castle

Industrious goblins, and a fateful fruit

Legends of dark deeds and supernatural beings cling to Scotland's castles like creeping ivy. Yester is a classic example, long famed for its secret subterranean chamber, said to have been built by a squad of hobgoblins conjured up by 13th-century laird Hugo de Giffard, a powerful wizard who used it to practise his occult magic.

As enchanted places go, it certainly looks the part. Perched on a precipitous tongue of rock, the castle itself was reduced centuries ago to gaunt ruins, now overgrown by tangled woodland worthy of a Grimm fairy tale. But Goblin Ha' [Hall], as the vaulted undercroft is known, remains in impressively good shape. A low, cramped tunnel serves as entrance to the loftily atmospheric expanse, which is lit only by two grated openings in the end wall, and has a steep inner staircase leading down (they say) to Hell.

Unlike many 'ancient' Scottish myths that turn out to be of quite recent coinage, the tale of the Wizard of Yester and his demonic builders has a respectably long pedigree. No less an authority than the 15th-century *Scotichronicon*, a history of early Scotland, includes a passage that recounts how Hugo's 'marvellous underground cavern' was 'wrought by witchcraft'. Much later, inveterate romantic Walter Scott embroidered the legend into a vivid narrative for his epic 1808 poem 'Marmion', which features a description of Hugo's mystical garb that would put the denizens of Hogwarts to shame.

Another curious story tells of the magic pear that Hugo gave his daughter Margaret on her marriage to George Broun of nearby Colstoun, which would guarantee their future prosperity if preserved intact. Kept in a silver box, it did the job for over 400 years until a descendant's newly pregnant wife, Elizabeth Mackenzie, yielded to a craving and took a bite. The pear shrivelled, and with it the family's fortunes, as ruin and disaster ensued.

Address Yester Estate, near Gifford, EH41 4PG | **Getting there** From Gifford village, take B 6355 and head south for 2.5 miles to Castle Park Golf Club (ask for permission to park). Walk round the perimeter of the golf course, with the dyke on your right, until you come to a gap in the fencing, where a path leads through woodland and up a steep embankment to the castle site | **Hours** Castle exterior always visible. Goblin Ha' is currently closed, due to safety concerns following thefts of stonework | **Tip** An ancient pear, said to be the very one gifted by Hugo, is preserved at Colstoun House by its umpteenth laird, Ludovic Broun-Lindsay. Although the enchanted fruit – reportedly the size of a walnut, and still bearing toothmarks – is not on view, decorative pear motifs are in evidence throughout the building.

18__Gullane Golf Club
Venerable turf with ace vistas

The charming village of Gullane (population 2,810) has a fame that transcends its modest size. This is based principally on three factors: its legendary poshness, the long-running debate over how to pronounce its name, and above all its hallowed status among devotees of the cult of golf. In a prime coastal site, midway along East Lothian's formidable string of links, it boasts no fewer than three classic courses within the bounds of the village itself, while a further two – Luffness and the illustrious Muirfield – occupy its southern and eastern approaches.

Links golf is generally said to be the purest form of the game, reflecting its origins as a knockabout medieval pastime: records show that 'the gowf' was being played on sand dunes around the Firth of Forth in the mid-15th century, when it was already popular with all social classes. Within East Lothian, Musselburgh has the course with the longest documented pedigree, dating from 1672, though an old tale claims that Mary, Queen of Scots played a few holes at nearby Seton in 1567.

Gullane's venerable Golf Club manages the village courses, known as numbers 1, 2 and 3 simply to indicate the order in which they were established. Each offers a highly memorable golfing experience in a stunning setting, though Gullane No. 1 is not only the oldest, dating from 1884, but the most renowned, regularly ranked among the best in Scotland. As with all traditional links courses, its ancient turf and undulating terrain were primarily shaped by nature rather than 'built' – and the panoramic views that it offers, across the Firth of Forth to Edinburgh and beyond, are truly spellbinding.

To return to the unresolved debate: true locals say 'Gullan' and posh incomers favour 'Gillan', though it's worth pointing out that 'Goollan' seems to have been the original pronunciation. Just don't ever call it 'Gull-ANE'.

Address West Links Road, Gullane, EH31 2BB, +44 (0)1620 842255, www.gullanegolfclub.co.uk | Getting there Bus 124 or X5 to Gullane (Goose Green) | Hours Daily; tee times bookable online, see website for availability and prices. Day tickets available in summer | Tip If you'd rather just enjoy a good walk unspoiled, grab an ice cream from the excellent Imma's Gelato at 10 Rosebery Place and head inland to Saltcoats Castle, an impressive ruin about half a mile south on Saltcoats Road. Alternatively, take the path up Gullane Hill that skirts the No. 1 course and continue down to Gullane Bents, one of East Lothian's finest beaches.

19_La Potinière

A legend in its own lunchtime

With its modest scale and domestic appearance, you could pass by La Potinière without realising it's even a restaurant, let alone one of the most celebrated icons of the industry in the whole of Scotland. 'The gossiping place', as the name translates, is a long-time fixture of Gullane's Main Street, dating back to the 1970s when David and Hilary Brown took over an old tearoom. Despite a lack of formal training, they succeeded in transforming the tiny premises into a unique venue for fine dining, gaining a loyal local following and eventually the coveted accolade of a Michelin star. Sunday lunch became so popular that bookings had to be made months in advance.

There was dismay when the couple moved on in 2002, but after a two-year hiatus the much-missed institution was reborn thanks to another husband-and-wife team, Keith Marley and Mary Runciman. Both experienced chefs, they brought their own style and expertise to the table, and before long had established themselves as more than worthy successors. Two decades on, the restaurant continues to win ecstatic plaudits, whether from gourmand reviewers or customers rhapsodising on online platforms.

There's a refreshing lack of pomp and pretension about the place. Its intimate proportions, unobtrusive décor, music-free ambience and discreet service all go towards focusing the attention on the simple appreciation of excellent food, prepared with consummate skill and perfectly cooked. The thoughtfully planned menu is limited to two choices per course, each based on fresh, top quality seasonal produce, locally sourced, including vegetables from the restaurant's own garden. Typical dishes include seared scallops with ham hock terrine; an exquisite take on Cullen Skink (traditional fish soup); braised lamb shank with rosemary-scented potatoes; and 'apple pizza' from award-winning *pâtissier* Keith. All this at a price that won't break the bank. Booking is, understandably, essential.

Address 34 Main Street, Gullane, EH31 2AA, +44 (0)1620 843214,
www.lapotiniere.co.uk | Getting there Bus 124 or X5 to Gullane (Maule Terrace) | Hours
Thu – Sat lunch 12.30pm & dinner 7pm, Sun lunch 12.30pm | Tip If you're in the market
for a luxury country-house experience in an idyllic, secluded setting, you'll love Greywalls
Hotel. Situated to the east of Gullane on the edge of Muirfield Golf Course, the cosily
elegant residence was built in 1901 as a holiday home for politician and sportsman Alfred
Lyttleton. It was designed by the celebrated Sir Edwin Lutyens and is surrounded by a six-
acre walled garden attributed to Gertrude Jekyll.

20 Amisfield Walled Garden

From preserve of the posh to asset for all

Just east of Haddington by the River Tyne is an expanse of verdant parkland with a surprising hidden history. Formerly known as New Mills, it was an early site of industry, used by nuns from the 12th-century abbey for fulling cloth, and later for grinding grain. In 1681 it became home to a 'great manufactory' of woollen fabric, an enterprise that ended in tragedy for its founder, Sir James Stanfield, when he was murdered by his wastrel eldest son, whom he had disinherited. Another reprobate entered the scene in 1713 – Colonel Francis Charteris, a notorious card sharp and convicted rapist, who used his ill-gotten gains to buy the estate, which he renamed Amisfield after his ancestral home in Dumfriesshire.

But it was his much more respectable grandson Francis, 7th Earl of Wemyss, who made a lasting impact on the site. A man of cultivated taste, he undertook a vast programme of improvement, building a Palladian-style mansion and remodelling the grounds as a 'designed landscape'. The house is long gone, and part of the estate is now a golf course, but some features survive, including a huge walled kitchen garden, dating from 1783. With 16-foot walls enclosing eight acres, paths laid out in Union Jack formation and a Neoclassical pavilion at each corner, it was designed to impress – as was its produce, such as pineapples, peaches and grapes, grown at staggering expense in 'pinery-vinery' hothouses.

The garden suffered decline and abandonment in the 20th century, but thanks to the sterling efforts of a host of local volunteers led by the Amisfield Preservation Trust, it is now being restored and completely redeveloped as a wonderful community asset, open to visitors free of charge. Training in horticulture is offered to people from every walk of life, plus the opportunity to enjoy the fruits of their labours – including tomatoes, courgettes and aubergines that would surely have wowed the 7th Earl.

Address Amisfield Park, Haddington, EH41 3TE, www.amisfield.org.uk | Getting there Bus X6, X7, 106, 108, 111, 111A, 121, 122 or 253 to Haddington town centre, then a one-mile walk: from Nungate area follow road to Golf Club, then path beyond clubhouse. Alternatively, join footpath along the north bank of the River Tyne at Riverside Drive, then cross river at Abbey Bridge | Hours Mon–Fri 10am–4pm, Sat 10am–1pm; see website or Facebook page for events and workshops | Tip Back in the town centre is another historic walled garden, St Mary's Pleasance, restored in the 1970s as a delightful green haven in 17th-century style.

21 __ The Cheese Lady
Championing a culture of natural goodness

The simple sign on the Haddington shopfront says it all. Such is the reputation earned by titular proprietor Svetlana Kukharchuk that what began as an affectionate nickname now ranks as a respectful honorific. She has become THE Cheese Lady *par excellence*. With lengthy and varied experience in the trade, her expertise in all things cheese, and evangelical passion for promoting its virtues, have won accolades from a growing customer base in East Lothian and beyond, as well as coveted awards from the retail and business communities.

Svetlana's cheese epiphany happened in (of all places) the USA, where she had relocated from her home in Siberia on a student exchange. Having suffered from an eating disorder in her teens, she was keen to learn more about proper nutrition, and was fascinated to discover the health benefits of natural, hand-crafted cheese, not to mention its delicious complexity and endless variety – worlds away from dull, industrially produced equivalents. After a spell as an intern at a New York cheesemongery, she headed to France to learn more about the subtle art of cheese ageing. Her personal life then took her to Fife, where she worked with a farmhouse cheese-maker, and in 2010 she realised a dream with the opening of her own shop in St Andrews. Seven years later the venture was reborn in Haddington as The Cheese Lady; such was its success that before long it needed larger premises, and it now boasts a maturing room as well as a tiny café.

Svetlana's expertly curated choice of fine cheeses from Europe and the British Isles demonstrates the extraordinary gamut of flavours, textures, aromas and styles that can be derived from cow, sheep or goat milk, by natural processes of transformation that seem quite magical. A range of condiments and crackers is also on sale, plus an intriguing selection of wines, beers and other drinks to complement your choice.

Address 3 Court Street, Haddington, EH41 3JD, +44 (0)1620 823729, www.thecheeselady.co.uk | Getting there Bus X6, X7, 101, 106, 108, 110, 111, 121, 122, 123 or 253 to Haddington town centre | Hours Tue–Sat 10am–5pm | Tip Another specialist Haddington food retailer that deserves your custom is the renowned Falko Konditorei, a long-established, premium-quality German bakery and café at 91 High Street.

22__Lennoxlove

Restoration romance and wartime intrigue

Lennoxlove is a name that resounds with romantic promise, so it's good to know that the person responsible for christening it was a colourful Restoration courtier famed for her beauty, Frances Teresa Stewart. Sad to relate, however, she never actually lived here. Dubbed 'La Belle Stuart' by one of her many admirers, Frances was the original model for Britannia on the coinage of Charles II, who was besotted with her. But Frances rebuffed his advances and eloped with his cousin, the Duke of Lennox. When she died childless in 1702 she left a bequest to her relative Lord Blantyre to enable him to buy the Scottish property, on condition that it was renamed in memory of her husband and their mutual devotion.

The house began life as the more prosaic Lethington, a fortified tower whose origins go back to 1345, when the land was acquired by the Maitland family, who went on to gain considerable power at the courts of the Stewart monarchs. Their massive keep survives as a key element of the building, which was extended over the centuries to create two contrasting wings: an elegant suite of rooms with Georgian interiors, designed for gracious living, and the castle-like chambers centred on the Great Hall. This atmospheric space was given an overhaul in 1912–14 by medievalist architect Robert Lorimer, who added the chunky chimneypiece, carved with heraldic beasts and mottoes, for new owner Major William Baird.

In 1946 Lennoxlove was bought by the 14th Duke of Hamilton, whose family art collection, including portraits by big names like Van Dyck and Raeburn, now fills its rooms. Two rather more unexpected items on display are a map and compass used in 1941 by Rudolf Hess, Hitler's deputy, on a bizarre solo flight to Scotland that ended in his arrest. Hess was rumoured to have been on a mission to see the duke, whom he had met before the war, in an attempt to initiate peace talks.

Address Near Haddington, EH41 4NZ, +44 (0)1620 823720, www.lennoxlove.com |
Getting there Visitor entrance on B 6369, half a mile south of Haddington; bus X 7 to
Haddington town centre and a 35-minute walk (including driveway) | **Hours** Guided
tours Apr–Oct, Wed, Thu, Sun noon, 1pm, 2pm & 3pm; online booking essential | **Tip**
The parkland around the house has been home since 1979 to the Cadzow White Cattle, a
magnificent, exceptionally rare breed thought to be descended from the auroch, or European
wild ox, and the only such herd in Scotland. Fiercely shy beasts with long upturned horns,
they can be admired at a distance but should on no account be approached.

23 __ St Mary's Parish Church
The Lamp of Lothian shines on

Haddington is blessed with a glorious medieval church that enjoys several rare distinctions – ample, cathedral-like proportions, an idyllic riverbank setting and warm, resonant acoustics, to cite just three. But perhaps the most remarkable is the triumph of its 20th-century resurrection, after 400 years when half the building had languished as a roofless shell.

St Mary's was founded in 1380, a quarter of a century after an English raid, graphically known as the Burnt Candlemas, had destroyed an earlier kirk on the site, along with a Franciscan church of such radiant beauty that it was referred to as the Lamp of Lothian. It took many decades to complete the replacement, in soaring Gothic style – but only months to reduce it to a semi-ruinous state. The culprit behind this ravaging was Henry VIII, whose troops laid siege to Haddington in 1548 during the 'Rough Wooing' – a queasy nickname for the war aimed at forcing a marriage between his son Edward and the infant Mary, Queen of Scots. The town could only afford a partial repair, and so in 1562 a partition wall was erected, separating off the devastated choir and transepts, with the nave alone restored as a parish kirk for Protestant worship.

It was not until the 1960s that a visionary plan emerged to re-roof and repair the ruined section and reunite the structure as a single entity. At first it was controversial, but after a successful fund-raising appeal led by the Duchess of Hamilton, the scheme went ahead in 1971, and was happily completed before the 1973 oil crisis and ensuing rampant inflation. A key feature was the innovative recreation of the original stone vaulting, ribs and bosses in lightweight fibreglass resin, work carried out by Lowestoft boatbuilders.

With its luminous splendour renewed for the benefit of the whole community, St Mary's now deservedly bears the historic mantle of the Lamp of Lothian.

Address Sidegate, Haddington, EH41 4BZ, www.stmaryskirk.co.uk | **Getting there** Bus X6, X7, 101, 106, 108, 110, 111, 121, 122, 123 or 253 to Haddington town centre | **Hours** May–Sept, Sat & Sun 1.30–4pm. Friendly volunteer guides are on hand to welcome visitors | **Tip** Classical music is an important part of the life of St Mary's. In September the church is one of the chief venues for the world-class Lammermuir Festival, and there are regular concerts throughout the year including a free series on spring and summer Sundays at 4pm.

24__The Waterside Bistro

Relax and dine by the timeless River Tyne

East Lothian is blessed with numerous idyllic corners, but against any competition the picture-postcard setting of the Waterside Bistro must rank among the most delightful in the whole county. In the historic Haddington district of Nungate, it occupies a neat row of whitewashed, red-pantiled, 19th-century cottages, beside the stone arches of the characterful bridge over the Tyne that has linked the two communities since medieval times. (The Nungate, incidentally, is a proud ancient barony with a distinctive identity, boasting its own annual gala day and even its own tartan.) There's outdoor seating right by the waterside, and a cosy interior with an attractively rustic feel and a welcoming log fire. Best of all is the matchless outlook, with swans gliding by on the river and vistas along its green banks of the town's majestic parish church, St Mary's.

Happily, the calibre of what's on offer at the Waterside amply measures up to the location when it comes to food, drink and hospitality. It's very much a family enterprise, now in the hands of James and Jack Findlay, who grew up next door to the bistro and took over its running in 2017. Their father Jim founded it back in 1982, when eateries of this kind and quality were a distinct rarity in these parts, and it soon became a local institution, attracting regular customers from all over the county and even appreciative *cognoscenti* from Edinburgh.

The emphasis is on fresh locally-sourced ingredients, with inventive cuisine for lighter appetites as well as popular favourites such as steak (from an award-winning Tranent butcher) and haddock and chips. There are always vegetarian options, daily specials and dishes for children, and you'll certainly want to leave room for one of the tempting homemade desserts. If it's just a quiet drink you're after, that's fine too – there's real ale from Haddington brewer Winton's and cider from Thistly Cross of Dunbar, as well as a good-value range of wines.

Address 1–5 Waterside, Haddington, EH41 4AT, +44 (0)1620 825674, www.thewatersidebistro.co.uk | **Getting there** Bus X6, X7, 101, 106, 108, 110, 111, 121, 122, 123 or 253 to Haddington town centre and short walk east | **Hours** Bar: Sun–Thu noon–10pm, Fri & Sat noon–11pm; kitchen: Mon–Thu noon–2.30pm & 5.30–8.30pm, Fri–Sun noon–8.30pm | **Tip** If you fancy a quiet walk before or after your meal, cross to the other side of the Nungate Bridge and take a stroll westwards along the river, past the church and up to Long Cram, where you'll see a variety of waterfowl.

25 Gosford House

I dreamt I dwelt in marble halls

To those who know East Lothian, it should come as no surprise to learn that one of its grandest stately homes owes its existence to an enduring passion for golf. It was the coastal dunes of this county that gave birth to the game, which by the late 15th century had become a craze at every level of society. Gosford was originally a breezy wasteland of sandy, rabbit-warrened turf – a perfect golf links – and early devotee King James V made regular use of a well-appointed tower on the isolated site as a clubhouse-cum-love-nest.

The need for fortified residences was long past by 1784, when art connoisseur and golf fanatic Francis Charteris, 7th Earl of Wemyss, bought the barony of Gosford and commissioned celebrated architect Robert Adam to create the swankiest pavilion imaginable, a place for refined entertaining with the links on its doorstep. Adam died not long after construction began, but the Neoclassical palace was completed in 1800 according to his plans. Meanwhile, the grounds were transformed into lush pleasure gardens, incorporating a curious mausoleum to which Francis was consigned on his own death in 1808. Like many upper echelon golfers of his day, he was a staunch Freemason, and the pyramidical tomb, surrounded by 16 yew trees, was designed on esoteric principles of numerology.

In the following 20 years the house was altered and clumsily shorn of its wings, but in the 1880s the 10th Earl (another art collector and golf nut) began a major programme of restoration. It was then that Gosford acquired its most breathtaking feature: the three-storey marble hall. It's an airily elegant Italianate space that seems quite incongruous in these northern climes, where even the tree belt that borders the western gate has been stunted into submission by centuries of chill, salty winds. But, like so much else in this remarkable place, it works like a dream.

Address Longniddry, EH32 0PX, +44 (0)1875 870808, www.gosfordhouse.co.uk | Getting there Bus 124, 125 or X5 to Gosford House main gate | Hours Apr–Aug: House tours on Open Days; see website for dates (booking essential). Grounds: open daily; permit required, obtainable from Estate Office (Mon–Fri 9am–5pm) or Farm Shop | Tip The well-stocked Gosford Bothy Farm Shop and Butchery is at the north-east corner of the estate, next to the grounds car park and just west of Aberlady. Much of their excellent produce comes from the estate, and most of the rest is locally sourced.

26 The Brunton

A modernist icon for community culture

Despite its situation just six miles from Edinburgh, Musselburgh has always been a distinctive community, a long-time rival of the capital that refuses to let itself be overshadowed by its uppish neighbour. This local identity is proudly displayed in the striking modernist theatre that has dominated the town since 1971. Originally known as the Brunton Memorial Hall, it opened at a time when the nearby Festival City was embroiled in a long-running farce about a proposed opera house that never saw the light of day – in fact its architect, William Kininmonth, had previously been engaged on the Edinburgh project, only to have his designs ultimately rejected as unworthy.

Musselburgh's showpiece owes its existence to local wireworks owner John Brunton, who left a substantial legacy to the town to provide a purpose-built hall for community cultural use. This was supplemented by the council so that it could be incorporated into a civic centre, housing offices for local services. As a focal point on the plain concrete façade, Kininmonth commissioned a work from Edinburgh sculptor Tom Whalen – a vast symbol-laden roundel in gilded bronze, depicting an exuberant sunburst hovering protectively above a recumbent nude figure. Now comprising two recently revamped state-of-the-art performance spaces, the Brunton has hosted many famous names over the years, from Billy Connolly and Barbara Dickson to Scottish Opera and the National Theatre of Scotland, while also supporting a variety of enterprising local arts organisations.

In March 2023 the much-loved venue fell victim to the UK-wide crumbling concrete crisis, and was forced to close both its theatres when they were judged potentially unsafe. But the Brunton Trust barely missed a beat, and while the building is being overhauled it continues to present its varied programme of shows from alternative venues in East Lothian.

Address Ladywell Way, Musselburgh, EH21 6AF, +44 (0)131 653 5254, www.thebrunton.co.uk. Temporary performance venues Northesk Parish Church (just across the road), Loretto Theatre, Musselburgh, EH21 7RE and the Corn Exchange, Haddington, EH41 3DS | **Getting there** Musselburgh venues: bus 26, 44, 46, 106, 113 or 124; Corn Exchange: bus X6, X7, 101, 106, 108, 110, 111, 121, 122, 123 or 253 | **Hours** See website for performances. Box office in Brunton building Mon–Fri 11am–3pm, also Sat 11am–3pm at Musselburgh Library | **Tip** Tranent has its own community arts venue, the Fraser Centre, which houses a lively programme of film screenings, drama and music, as well as activities including craft and dance classes. There's also a popular café, open Tue–Sat 9am–3pm.

27 Inveresk Lodge Garden
A breath of fresh air

The leafy conservation village of Inveresk stands on a high ridge above the coastal town of Musselburgh – just 15 minutes' walk from the bustle of the High Street, but worlds away in its affluent seclusion. As a site for upmarket dwellings, its origins go back nearly two millennia, when there was a comfortable Roman township here, equipped with baths and central heating. Much later, it became a favoured resort of the 18th-century Edinburgh gentry escaping from the crowded, noisome capital. They replaced the humble cottages of the single-street rural village with a series of showy villas, set within spacious gardens that made the most of the fertile soil and sunny slopes, all screened from view by high stone walls. In later decades this enclave – famed for its 'salubrious air and beauteous prospect', to quote local poet David Macbeth Moir – gained the soubriquet 'Scotland's Montpellier'.

Inveresk Lodge is one the earliest mansions in the village. Built at the end of the 17th century, it was donated to the National Trust for Scotland in 1959, together with its 13-acre garden, by the Brunton family, industrialists whose generosity also funded the construction of Musselburgh's theatre. Though the house is closed to the public, the garden is open every day of the year, and after you've passed the long stretch of private properties on the way, it seems a huge privilege to be allowed access.

The first section, centred on an elaborate 17th-century sundial, is conceived in Arts and Crafts style as a series of 'garden rooms', each planted with a different theme designed to be at its colourful best in a particular season. Another enjoyable feature is the Edwardian glasshouse, just inside the entrance. From this formality, grassy slopes lead down to extensive woodland dotted with fecund apple trees and meadows interspersed with ponds, where you may well spot deer and other wildlife. Remarkably, the entire vast and gloriously refreshing expanse is managed by a single gardener.

Address 24 Inveresk Village Road, Musselburgh, EH21 7TE | Getting there Bus 26, 44, 108 or X26 to Musselburgh (King Street) and a short uphill walk, or 111/A, 140, 141 or X6 to Inveresk village | Hours Daily Apr–Sept 10am–5pm, Jan–Mar 10am–4.30pm | Tip The delightful Shepherd House Garden is a minute's walk away on Crookston Road. A private one-acre garden developed over more than 50 years by botanical painter Lady Ann Fraser and her husband, it's open regularly to the public in aid of charity, via the Scotland's Gardens Scheme.

28__Luca's

Serving scoops of delight for three generations

Musselburgh folk are living proof of the adage that it's never too cold for ice cream. Whatever the season, and however unseasonable the weather, the institution that is Luca's café welcomes a constant stream of local customers, as it has done for nearly 120 years, to savour the cool, sweet dairy treat, freshly made on the premises to a time-honoured family recipe. These days it's available in a vast range of gourmet flavours – though vanilla is still the number one choice.

The story of one of the most esteemed Italian ice-cream dynasties in Scotland goes back to the 1890s, when young Luca Scappaticcio left the poverty of his native Cassino and emigrated to Edinburgh. He found work in the kitchens of the North British Hotel, where a Swiss pastry chef taught him the art that became his trade. By 1908 he and his new wife Anastasia had saved enough to open their own ice-cream parlour, which they named the Olympia, along the coast in Musselburgh. As if the work of making the stuff wasn't hard enough in those pre-refrigeration days, the couple initially had to walk there and back every day from their home in the city centre.

With all their children working with them from an early age, the business thrived and grew over the years to encompass a busy wholesale trade, additional cafés and roving ice-cream vans (including a special-occasion converted Rolls-Royce, reputedly bought from a Spanish nobleman). When in time son Tino took over, the family brand became known as S. Luca, their actual surname being judged too much of a mouthful for Scots, and today two third-generation Lucas, Michael and Yolanda, run their grandfather's empire. Still on the original site, the café has recently benefitted from a makeover inside and out, with swish glazed brick and jaunty tiling that stylishly evoke the continuing company ethos of traditional quality for the 21st century.

Address 32–38 High Street, Musselburgh, EH21 7AG, +44 (0)131 665 2237, www.lucasicecream.co.uk | Getting there Bus 106, 113, 124, 125 to Luca's or 26, 44, 48, 108, 111, 140, 141, X6 or X26 to Newbigging | Hours Daily, takeaway 9am–10pm, café 9am–8.30pm (last orders 8pm) | Tip If you fancy a preface to your Knickerbocker Glory, Banana Split or Chocolate Nut Sundae, the sit-in café has an extensive menu of savoury favourites including homemade pizza and pasta dishes (the macaroni cheese is deservedly popular) as well as burgers, salads, soup, sandwiches and all-day breakfast choices.

29 Pinkie House Ceiling

A rare brush with Renaissance philosophy

The Renaissance: that great rebirth of classical learning and culture, it all happened in Italy, surely! Well, yes and no. Scotland was late to the party that got going in the early 14th century, but like every other country in Europe it saw its own flowering of intellectual and artistic life as the game-changing new ideas gradually travelled north. This nation had its fair share of churches packed with altarpieces and statuary before the cataclysm of the 16th-century Reformation; in its wake, however, a new secular tradition took shape as Scottish artists turned to decorating the homes of the aristocracy. A fashion emerged for elaborate ceilings, painted with imagery from classical mythology and literature, intended to show off the patron's learning.

One of the finest surviving examples is the 79-foot-long Painted Gallery at Pinkie House, a palatial mansion built in 1613 by the Lord Chancellor of Scotland, Alexander Seton. Having spent seven years as a student in Rome, Seton was steeped in the humanist culture of the European élite. The ceiling he commissioned is an ambitiously epic scheme, designed to give the illusion of a spacious aisle, with cupolas open to the sky and a series of paintings hung around the vault. Inscribed with Latin mottoes, these depict narratives illustrating the ideals of Neo-Stoic philosophy, which advocated self-discipline and virtuous living. One features Seton himself as a personification of moderation, while another includes a group of decidedly unstoical nymphs and satyrs enjoying a merry dance. Regrettably, the original *trompe l'oeil* quality was reduced by conservation work in the 1970s, which altered the texture of the lean tempera paint and darkened the colours.

Since 1951 Pinkie House has been part of Loretto School. The Gallery is now used for exams; whether it's an inspiration or a distraction for pupils is unclear.

Address Loretto School, Linkfield Road, Musselburgh, EH21 7AF, www.loretto.com | Getting there Bus 106, 113, 124 or 125 to Luca's or 26, 44, 48, 108, 111, 140, 141, X6 or X26 to Newbigging | Hours Contact the school to enquire about visiting Pinkie House – guided tours are sometimes available | Tip To learn more about the history of the 'Honest Toun', visit Musselburgh's welcoming little museum at 65 High Street. Staffed by local volunteers, it has both permanent displays and changing exhibitions covering a fascinating variety of topics on the life of the community, from the earliest times up to the present day.

30___Auld Kirk Green

Fake news from Scotland, 1590s-style

On a pocket of grass near North Berwick harbour stands a ruinous stone porch, flanked by low, fragmentary rubble walls. Bypassed by most of today's carefree trippers, these are the sad remains of the early medieval Kirk of St Andrew, a magnet for the tourists of the Middle Ages – pilgrims, *en route* to the miraculous shrine at St Andrews, who stopped to pray, and to stay in neighbouring hostels, before taking the ferry across to Fife.

The 16th-century Reformation and its censure of the cult of relics brought an end to this lucrative traffic. But darker superstitions now came to the fore, and in the 1590s the kirk became mired in dangerous intrigue, as the alleged base of a coven of witches who had used sorcery to plot against King James VI. A fancifully illustrated pamphlet, published in London with the laconic title *Newes from Scotland*, gave a sensational account of the first trials that ensued. The most vivid confession, from Agnes Sampson, a midwife and healer, told how she and 200 others had caroused with the devil one night in the kirkyard and conjured up a storm at sea, aimed at sinking the ship in which James and his new queen were then returning from Denmark. The king himself took part in her trial, which involved vile torture, culminating in the grim charade of pricking her naked body to reveal the 'devil's mark'. Around 70 other innocent individuals were similarly persecuted, and many, like Agnes, were executed by strangulation at the stake followed by burning.

With the royal seal of approval, the infamous North Berwick trials acted as a catalyst for the hideous campaign of witch hunts that followed in both Scotland and England (where James acceded to the throne in 1603), and led to the conviction and death of thousands, mainly women. As for the kirk, it was abandoned in 1656 after part of the building was swept away in another maritime storm.

27 Victoria Road, North Berwick, EH39 4JL | Train to North Berwick and a 15-minute walk; bus 120, 121 to Seabird Centre or 124, X5 to Church Road | The porch houses a small, informative display, open daily | St Andrew's Kirk Ports, the church built in the 1660s to replace the Old Kirk, is a few minutes' walk away, on a peaceful green site just behind the busy High Street. In the 1870s it was left to decline into a 'picturesque ruin', having been superseded in its turn by a third Church of St Andrew.

31 The Bass Rock

Shimmering citadel of the Solan goose

Looming large on the horizon east of North Berwick is the unmistakable rock known simply as the Bass. With sheer cliffs rising 350 feet out of the sea, it's the most formidable of the Firth of Forth islands, though its chunky profile and distinctive paleness may evoke thoughts of a giant scone to some flippant landlubbers.

The Bass originated in the vent of an ancient volcano, as a plug of molten magma that cooled to form dark crystalline rock. Its change in hue is all down to Britain's largest seabird, the Northern gannet – countless generations have made their seasonal home on its precipitous terrain. Despite the recent ravages of avian flu, the Bass is still the world's biggest gannetry, with a 150,000-strong, highly vocal colony of these no-nonsense, sharp-beaked birds, jostling and bonding on the cramped nesting sites, swooping, soaring and deftly folding their six-foot wingspan to plummet torpedo-style in pursuit of fish. When viewed from afar, the myriad dots of white plumage and guano-streaked crag merge to create a shimmering jewel surmounted by an ethereal halo.

Once known as Solan geese, the gannets of the Bass have attracted considerable interest for many centuries, though until as late as the 1850s this was far from benign. The eggs and fledgling birds were popular delicacies (said to taste best with generous quaffs of sherry), and barrels of gannet fat were sold for use in medicine and as a lubricant. In today's more enlightened times, mini-cruises round the rock allow visitors a privileged window on these birds' extraordinary lives, and landing excursions are also possible. Spending time in the midst of the gannet multitudes is an immersive experience for all the senses that's like setting foot on another world. Evidence of a long history of human occupation – the ruins of a castle, chapel and prison, plus a fine lighthouse – can also be seen, but these seem oddly out of place. There's no question whose rock it is now.

Address Firth of Forth; accessible from the Harbour, North Berwick, EH39 4JW | Getting there Mini-cruises round the Bass are run by Sula Boat Trips (+44 (0)1620 849289, www.sulaboattrips.co.uk) and the Scottish Seabird Centre (+44 (0)1620 890202, www.seabird.org); the Seabird Centre also offers guided landing trips | Hours Mini-cruises: Apr – Sept daily, sailing times vary | Tip Right next to the *Sula* booking office on North Berwick harbour is the Lobster Shack, a popular local institution offering a choice selection of sustainably fished seafood, cooked to order.

32 Coastal Communities Museum

Land, sea, people and stories

The stunning seafront and characterful old centre of North Berwick have so much to offer that many visitors hardly stray beyond them. But there's one attraction just off the beaten track that anyone curious about the past life and times of this enchanting town should definitely add to their itinerary. Unobtrusively housed in a suite of rooms above the local library, the Coastal Communities Museum is an absolute gem, an exemplar of its kind that's all the more remarkable for being entirely staffed by volunteers. It's a genuine community enterprise, opened in 2013 after a hard-won campaign following the closure in 2002 of the council-run museum that used to occupy the site.

The museum today is a bright, attractive space designed to appeal to all ages, where you're greeted by friendly, enthusiastic guides. The carefully researched displays cover a wide gamut of intriguing subjects relating to the social history and natural heritage of North Berwick and its surroundings; stand-out exhibits include the original optics from the Bass Rock lighthouse and the two-seater 17th-century town stocks, and there are fascinating insights into the diverse lives of former generations, from fishermen to doctors to the female farmworkers known as bondagers.

You'll also learn about Catherine Watson, a talented 19-year-old artist who met a tragic end in 1889 while rescuing a child from drowning in East Bay, and Aeneas Piccolomini, the future Pope Pius II, who in the winter of 1435 made a punishing barefoot pilgrimage from Dunbar to the snowbound Holy Well at Whitekirk, while on a diplomatic mission to the court of James I. Some 70 years later, his miserable Scottish sojourn was fancifully reimagined by Renaissance artist Pinturicchio, in a charming fresco for Siena Cathedral.

Address School Road, North Berwick, EH39 4JU, +44 (0)1620 894313, www.coastalmuseum.org | **Getting there** Train to North Berwick and a 20-minute walk; bus 120 or 121 to Seabird Centre, or 124 or X5 to Church Road | **Hours** Apr–Oct, Wed–Sat 11am–4pm | **Tip** The museum has an excellent series of leaflets on local places of interest. Well worth seeking out while you're in the east of the town is the Glen, a secluded woodland with a burn running through it and the ruins of a 16th-century mill. It was landscaped in Victorian times to create the Ladies Walk, a pathway designed for picturesque effect.

33___Drift Café

Bliss out over brunch

'Eat, drink, relax' is the welcoming motto that greets customers at Drift – though the real-estate mantra 'Location, location, location' would also ring true. Perched on a clifftop along the coast from North Berwick amid thickets of sea buckthorn, this easy-going eatery has a panoramic outlook that's little short of magical. In a more mundane setting, a café made from half a dozen repurposed shipping containers might not be the most enticing place to linger, however tasty the fare. But for such a glorious site these vast crates, discreetly clad in larch, were an inspired architectural solution. As well as minimising the building's impact on the environment, they've also neatly lent themselves to conversion into a tranquil, light-filled space; floor-to-ceiling windows allow uninterrupted vistas up the coast and across the Firth of Forth, with the mesmerising Bass Rock at centre stage.

Opened in June 2018, Drift is the creation of farmers Stuart and Jo McNicol from nearby Castleton. The couple explored other agritourism projects before deciding on this scenic headland, formerly used for rough grazing, as the ideal site for a seaside café with a difference, convenient for motorists and bus travellers as well as walkers and cyclists. They started simply, with coffee and homemade cakes, and as their popularity grew so did the business; a second kitchen was soon added, along with a much expanded menu featuring freshly prepared brunch and lunch dishes, all based on seasonal, locally sourced produce. Potato crates were ingeniously turned into sheltered outdoor seating, and a converted horse box used as a takeaway trailer.

Drift's upbeat address, Canty Bay, is highly appropriate, canty being a Scots word meaning 'cheerful'. Adding further to the blissed-out mood is the golden strand to the west, Quarrel Sands, whose surly sounding name is just an old variant of quarry.

Address Canty Bay, North Berwick, EH39 5PL, +44 (0)1620 8932817, www.driftalong.co.uk | **Getting there** Bus 120 from North Berwick or Dunbar | **Hours** Daily 9.30am – 4.30pm, last orders 4pm | **Tip** Back in North Berwick town centre, coffee connoisseurs should seek out Steam Punk Coffee Roasters at 49a Kirk Ports for their exceptional quality beans. For excellent sourdough bread and unrivalled pâtisserie, visit Bostock Bakery at 42 High Street.

34 ___ The Jawbone Arch
Iconic reminder of the Arctic cowboys

The geological wonder that locals know simply as the Law rises abruptly from the upper reaches of North Berwick, like a sudden peak on a sales graph. Formed 350 million years ago as a plug of volcanic magma, then sculpted into a cone by glaciers of a later aeon, the 614-foot hill boasts exceptional 360-degree views, and an array of monuments and look-out points grace the summit. Two ruinous buildings serve as reminders of historic conflicts – an observation post used in both world wars, and a signal station from 1803, when a French invasion was thought to be imminent. The crowning glory, however, is an elegant 16-foot arch, a replica in fibreglass of an original made from whale jawbones. The previous, 70-year-old arch – the last in a series that had stood on Berwick Law for three centuries – was removed by the council in 2005 due to safety concerns. Locals became increasingly dismayed by its absence, until in 2008 a local businessman paid for the creation of a copy in weather-resistant materials, which was delivered by helicopter.

Commercial whaling by Scottish vessels in Arctic waters began in medieval times, and in the 18th and 19th centuries it was a vital part of the Scottish economy – whale oil was in constant demand for lighting, heating, soap and jute processing, and the bone had myriad uses, notably in the fashion industry. It was a dangerous business: whalers were nicknamed 'Arctic cowboys', and jawbones were often kept as a triumphal indicator of a successful hunt.

Though the glorification of this mass slaughter is sickening to modern sensibilities, arches made from the jaw of the bowhead whale (which has the largest mouth of any animal) were once a common sight in ports, and in the gardens of grand houses. North Berwick's popular hilltop icon is said to have acted as a landmark for sailors, though there's no other evidence that the town was ever involved in the whaling industry.

Address Berwick Law, North Berwick, EH39 4EZ | Getting there Train to North Berwick
and a 20-minute walk; bus 121 or 124 to Wishart Avenue, then follow the path from
Berwick Law Car Park, off B 1347 (c. 30 minutes to the top) | Tip A group of eight Exmoor
ponies, kept to graze the site and aid the growth of wild flowers, can often be spotted on the
lower slopes of the Law. Though undeniably cute, they are wild creatures – walkers should
keep their distance and under no circumstances try to feed them.

35 NB Distillery
Heady spirit of success

It could be the plot of a feelgood film. One evening in 2011, at home in the charming seaside town of North Berwick, Viv and Steve Muir are chatting over G & Ts when they're inspired to have a go at making their own gin. Both are corporate lawyers, with no experience of distilling or the drinks industry, but they're well aware that a renaissance is underway for the once-derided spirit. Starting in their kitchen with a contraption made from an old pressure cooker and central heating pipes, they spend thousands of hours perfecting the recipe. After trying out 200 botanicals they settle on a blend of eight, and finally invest in a handsome copper still, built to their specifications by the legendary firm of John Dore and christened 'Gloria'.

When the lovingly crafted small-batch NB Gin is launched in 2013 they can scarcely keep up with demand, which goes way beyond the anticipated local market. Soon it's stacking up awards, culminating in 2015 with World's Best London Dry Gin, while being quaffed at exclusive glitterati events and even earning a coveted place on the late Queen's drinks trolley. With Viv's brother Steve Ross as Head Distiller, the company expands in 2018 into purpose-built premises in a glorious rural setting, now equipped with a second bespoke still for creating the NB take on the latest fashionable tipple, rum.

The stylish eco-building was designed with tours in mind, and like so much else about this remarkable business, the visitor experience is a carefully considered and highly enjoyable combination of luxury and low-key. Following the maxim 'learn, sample, relax', the friendly, knowledgeable guides give you ample opportunity to do all three, with fascinating insights into processes and ingredients, plus generous draughts from their growing range, including the unique Samphire Gin, to sip and savour in the comfortable tasting lounge.

Address Halflandbarns, North Berwick, EH39 5PW, +44 (0)7511 103637, www.nbdistillery.com | Getting there Tours: Tue – Sat 5pm; booking essential | Hours Off A 198, half a mile beyond Tantallon Castle; bus 120 from North Berwick or Dunbar to Auldhame Cottages | Tip If single malt whisky is to your taste, take a tour of the atmospheric Glenkinchie Distillery, near Pencaitland. Founded in 1825, it also houses a small museum of whisky distilling. As well as being bottled under the Glenkinchie name, its floral Lowland malt is one of the ingredients of the Johnnie Walker blend.

36 The Seabird Centre

Zoom in on a world of maritime wonder

Of all the projects funded by the Millennium Commission to celebrate the year 2000, few can claim an impact to match that of the Scottish Seabird Centre. Having fulfilled its goal as a focus for regeneration of North Berwick's harbour area, the multi-award-winning attraction has gone on to become a vital force in local marine conservation, educating and inspiring countless thousands over the past quarter of a century with its increasingly urgent work.

Perched on a rocky promontory with open vistas of the Firth of Forth, the Centre is a heart-lifting sight, with its angular roofline expressively reaching for the sky. Inside, past a display on the horrors of plastic pollution and a shop with nature-focused books and gifts, you'll find a popular café with an outdoor terrace that on a sunny day is one of the most exhilarating places to be in all East Lothian.

But you have to spend time in the spacious basement gallery to experience the feature that was the Centre's innovative *raison d'etre* – the opportunity to watch seabirds remotely in their colonies on the outlying islands, via large screens connected to discreetly placed cameras, with interactive controls that allow you to zoom in and pan around as you please. The waterproof, solar-powered webcams are equipped with windscreen wipers, so there's always something to see: depending on the season it might be gannets feeding their chicks on the Bass Rock, puffins on Craigleith returning to their burrows, or grey seals lounging on the shores of the Isle of May. This real-time viewing is complemented by engrossing displays, games and interactives exploring marine wildlife and habitats, with an immersive presentation on bird migration that will leave you awestruck. Expert staff are on hand to deepen your appreciation of marine ecology, and of the many challenges that pose an ongoing threat to its health.

Wildlife to look out for...

Puffins returning to their
burrows on Fidra and
Craigleith in Spring

Thousands of seabirds
feeding their chicks on
the islands in Summer

Gannets fledging from
Bass Rock and grey
seals pupping in Autumn

Wading birds feeding
along the shoreline
in Winter

Address The Harbour, North Berwick, EH39 4SS, +44 (0)1620 890202, www.seabird.org |
Getting there Train to North Berwick and a 15-minute walk; bus 120 or 121 to Seabird
Centre or 124 or X5 to Church Road | Hours Daily, Jan, Nov & Dec 10am–4pm, Feb, Mar,
Sept & Oct 10am–5pm, Apr–Aug 10am–6pm | Tip The Centre offers seasonal cruises
round the seabird-rich sites of the Bass Rock, Craigleith and the Lamb (an uninhabited
island owned, intriguingly, by spoon-bending illusionist Uri Geller), plus landing trips to the
Isle of May, and a varied programme of family-focused outdoor activities and events.

37 Tantallon Castle

Mighty red fortress of the mighty Red Douglases

Forget Edinburgh's over-touristed citadel – if you want to see a castle with a copper-bottomed wow factor, head for Tantallon. Though ruinous and long uninhabited, its stunning location and uniquely powerful presence are guaranteed to make the heart race.

Boldly set on a high, narrow headland jutting into the Firth of Forth, this is a fortress that was certainly intended to daunt. Its massive rose-tinted curtain wall forms a titanic barrier on its landward approach, and 100-foot sheer cliffs plunge to the sea round its remaining sides, making further defences almost unnecessary. This effective impregnability gave rise to an old East Lothian saying, 'Ding doon Tantallon, mak a brig to the Bass' – a rough equivalent of 'pigs might fly', meaning that knocking it down was as impossible a feat as bridging the mile of sea that separates it from the Bass Rock.

Tantallon was built in the mid-14th century by William, 1st Earl of Douglas, a formidable figure in Scottish politics whose extramarital exploits resulted in a complicated family tree, with rival 'Black' and 'Red' branches. It was the latter who took over the castle in the 1380s, and it remained with the Red line for 300 years. Though it's not obvious today, it wasn't just a defensive stronghold but a comfortable residence for the nobility, featuring a seven-storey tower of apartments and a grandly furnished great hall. A lonely doocot (pigeon house) survives as a memory of their feasting. Many tried and failed to 'ding it doon' before Oliver Cromwell's artillery finally breached the walls in 1651.

Queen Victoria came here in August 1878, in weather that she described as 'extremely wild'. Undeterred, she took tea, seated on a sofa perched on a convenient ledge of rock. You can't do that today, sadly, but for an equally memorable experience, take a walk along the vertiginous parapets instead.

Address Near North Berwick, EH39 5PN, +44 (0)1620 892727, www.historicenvironment.scot/visit-a-place/places/tantallon-castle | **Getting there** Bus 120 from North Berwick or Dunbar | **Hours** Daily, Apr–Sept 9.30am–5pm, Oct–Mar 10am–4pm | **Tip** Of the Lothian region's many ruined fortresses, the most surprising must be Crichton Castle, which stands on a lonely hillside above the River Tyne near the Midlothian village of Pathhead. Its unexpected glory is a splendid interior courtyard, with an Italianate arched colonnade and walls covered with deeply carved diamond-shaped facets, thought to have been inspired by the Renaissance Palazzo dei Diamanti in Ferrara.

38_ The Great Yew

Arboreal marvel and witness to history

Any tree of great antiquity is a source of wonder, but ancient yews have a special mystique all of their own. These unique evergreens are exceptional survivors: thanks to their extraordinary ability to regenerate, it's not unusual for them to live for several centuries. Moreover, as members of the oldest tree genus in Europe, dating back 230 million years, even stripling yews could be classed as living fossils. In both material and spiritual terms, the yew has held a significant place in human culture since time immemorial, prized for its strong, flexible wood, esteemed for its medicinal properties and hallowed as a symbol of everlasting life and rebirth. Some claim it as the original Yggdrasil, the immense, sacred World Tree of Norse cosmology.

East Lothian is fortunate indeed to have two magnificent yews within its borders that are thought to be at least 1,000 years old, one on the Whittingehame Estate and the other in the grounds of the ruined Ormiston Hall. The Great Yew of Ormiston must already have been sizeable by 1474, when it was first recorded as a landmark. It's a splendid example of a 'layering' yew, with a vault-like array of branches that radiate from the beautifully fluted trunk to form a densely entwined canopy, then dip to the ground, where they've taken root and sprouted new growth. The core tree is thus surrounded by a green fringe of ever-extending 'bushes' that conceal the spacious inner chamber, giving it the feel of a secret refuge.

Countless meetings and ceremonies must have taken place over the centuries in this venerable enclave, though none perhaps as consequential as the sermon preached at Christmas 1545 by influential Protestant reformer George Wishart, in the company of his associate John Knox. Wishart was arrested shortly afterwards at the laird of Ormiston's house, taken to St Andrews, and subsequently burnt at the stake as a dangerous heretic.

Address Ormiston Hall, EH35 5NJ, OS grid reference NT41206761 | **Getting there** From A 6093, at 100 yards SW of junction with B 6371 take the lane leading south until you reach a ruined gateway and modern house on the right. Park here with consideration for residents. Continue for 25 yards, then turn right on to a path marked by two tree stumps | **Tip** An unusual cairn-like monument from World War II stands by the side of the lane, featuring a Polish eagle and Scottish lion rampant incised into a cement panel along with the date 15 August 1942 (Polish Armed Forces Day). It was built by Polish soldiers of the 10th Supply Company who were stationed in the grounds of Ormiston Hall, to commemorate the death of one of their number.

39 Preston Cross

Cornering the market for four centuries

Though now amalgamated into the cluster of communities that make up Prestonpans, the old village of Preston retains striking vestiges of its 17th-century heyday. It began life as the medieval 'priests' town', property of the industrious monks of Newbattle, and by 1617 had grown into a prosperous burgh of barony, with the newly granted right to hold a weekly market and annual fair. This status was marked by the erection of a handsome mercat (market) cross in warm yellow sandstone, carved with cutting-edge classical decoration; it stands to this day on its original site, impressively well preserved after four centuries of exposure. Some 126 mercat crosses survive in Scotland's old market towns, but many are rehashed affairs in a sad state of disrepair. Preston's is one of the very few in good condition that haven't been relocated – though its surroundings have changed beyond recognition.

'Cross' is a misleading name, for these monuments were very rarely cruciform. Their function was civic and secular, marking a formally sanctioned place for trade and the sale of goods. But they were much more besides, acting as a focal point for the community, where jostling crowds would gather to hear proclamations, take part in celebrations and enjoy amusements (including the public humiliation of wrong-doers).

Preston's cross is not only elegant but ingeniously multi-functional. The ground-floor drum houses a single-cell jail, plus a narrow staircase leading to an expansive platform for the town crier, while its exterior is furnished with six comfortable seats (try them!), in niches carved with scallop-shell motifs. Above is a towering column crowned with a pert little unicorn – Scotland's heraldic animal. With his sinuous form and curlicue-tipped shield, he bears a distinct resemblance to a seahorse, long since left high and dry but still proudly overseeing his domain.

Address Preston Road, Prestonpans, EH32 9PX | Getting there Bus 26, 111 or 124 to Preston Road (Health Centre) | Hours Viewable from the outside only | Tip Several other notable 17th-century buildings can be seen nearby, including Preston Tower and its lectern-style doocot, Northfield House and its beehive-shaped doocot, and Hamilton House (all viewable from the outside only). The village of Ormiston has a rare pre-Reformation mercat cross with an actual cross-shaped finial, thought to have been rescued from a demolished chapel.

40 Prestongrange Museum

Ghosts of industry in a quiet green haven

It's all too easy for travellers on the coast road between Musselburgh and Prestonpans to bypass the open-air museum at Prestongrange, shrouded as it is in banks of woodland. But those who do seek it out are in for an unusually memorable day out. In an area more associated with seaside leisure pursuits, the heritage park offers the chance to explore the monumental relics of what was once one of the most important industrial centres in Scotland. The tranquillity of the site – a green enclave where nature now holds sway – makes the experience particularly haunting.

Prestongrange is at the hub of a landscape rich in natural resources, chief among them coal, which was exploited as early as the 12th century, by the monks who owned the land, to boil sea water for the manufacture of salt. Fired by continuing improvements in mining technology, the locality developed over the next few hundred years into a prototype industrial estate, with a brickworks, potteries, glassworks and other specialist factories clustered around the all-important colliery, plus an on-site railway and a nearby harbour for the export of goods. By the early 20th century more than 1,000 people were employed here, but in 1962 it all came to an end with the colliery's closure.

The story might have ended there had it not been for the vision of retired mining engineer David Spence, who was instrumental in the preservation of the structures that form the core of the museum, at a time when the concept of industrial heritage was in its infancy. Among the most striking are the starkly sculptural winding gear that stood at the pit head, and a gigantic beam engine – an impressive steam-powered contraption used to pump water from the mine – dating from 1874. Vivid interpretation is on hand, from guides in person as well as audio tours, and the site is continually being developed with newly restored exhibits.

Address Morrison's Haven, Prestonpans, EH32 9RX, +44 (0)131 653 2904, www.eastlothian.gov.uk/info/210593/museums | Getting there Bus 26 or X26 to Morrison's Haven | Hours Apr–Sept, Wed–Sun 11am–4.30pm | Tip Nearby Wallyford is a village built on industry – three coal mines were once in operation here as well as a brick factory. An information board on Salters Road, opposite the junction with Drummohr Avenue, has a map showing local places of interest. These include two poignant memorial stones, one to the 38 men who lost their lives in the pits, and the other overlooking the site of the Battle of Pinkie Cleugh, the last pitched battle between England and Scotland, which took place on 10 September 1547, a day long remembered as Black Saturday.

41 Prestonpans Battlefield

Charlie is my darling

The battle for which Bonnie Prince Charlie is best remembered today is, sadly, Culloden, site of his harrowing last stand and now a popular tourist destination. By contrast, the opening engagement of the 1745 Jacobite rising, at Prestonpans, is relatively little known, despite its momentous outcome – a resounding victory for the young Stuart prince and his Highland clansmen against the Redcoats of King George II. After less than 20 minutes of 'action', the Jacobites were in control of Scotland. One incidental effect of the alarm that this caused in London was the rapid adoption of the patriotic song *God Save the King* as a proto-national anthem.

Despite modern development, much of the battleground has survived as open land, though it was not until 2006 that a charitable trust was set up to protect the site, tell the story of the battle and promote its legacy. As a stage towards their goal of creating a living history centre, they've recently opened an absorbing little museum in the old Prestonpans Town Hall, where events include regular costumed interpretation days. On the anniversary each September the battlefield hosts a full-scale two-day re-enactment, but if you can't make it then you'll still find much to explore and ponder on the walking trail around its varied landmarks and monuments. One of the later encroachments on the site, a large coal bing (spoil heap), was landscaped into a pyramid in the 1960s and now serves as a commanding viewpoint, with comprehensive information panels.

Two of the most evocative spots are those near Bankton House, home of the battle's most famous casualty, Colonel James Gardiner: a refurbished doocot, whose rather spooky interior houses a display on his life and times, and a memorial obelisk flanked by sleepy lions, erected in 1853 by the railway line to catch the eye of Victorian tourists on their way to Edinburgh.

Address For details of the battlefield trail, including a downloadable app, see www.battleofprestonpans1745.org. Museum: High Street, Prestonpans, EH32 9AY | **Getting there** Train to Prestonpans; bus 26, 111 or 124; the trail is signposted from outside the station exit on platform 2 | **Hours** Always accessible, except Bankton Doocot: daily 10am–6pm. Museum: Sat & Sun 11am–4pm | **Tip** Inspired by the famous exemplar in Bayeux, the 345-foot-long Prestonpans Tapestry (actually an embroidery, in wool on linen) tells the story of the battle. Stitched by more than 200 volunteers to a design by Andrew Crummy, it was completed in 2010 and has since been widely exhibited to great acclaim. Though as yet it has no permanent home, sections are on changing display in the museum.

42 Prestonpans Public Art
Creative reinvention of a post-industrial town

Though it's hard to credit today, the old burgh of Prestonpans was a hotbed of industry for over 900 years. Originally a fishing hamlet, it developed in early medieval times as a centre of salt making and coal mining, while the 18th century saw the growth of brewing, pottery, glass and brick manufacture. But the mid-20th century brought the collapse of all these traditional industries, followed by a sad decline.

Most of the remnants of this heritage had long since been swept away when, in 2003, an inspiring scheme was initiated to revive community pride through public art. Taking its lead from a famous project in the Canadian village of Chemainus, Prestonpans reinvented itself as Scotland's Mural Town. Over the next few years a team of artists led by Andrew Crummy worked with community groups and schools to create a trail of over 30 vibrant wall paintings in locations from shops to sports clubs, celebrating long-gone trades, industries and personalities, and depicting key moments from the area's history. One particularly striking image is Tom Ewing's darkly baroque *Witch!*, which regularly serves as a backdrop for open-air dramas based on the infamous East Lothian witch trials of the 1590s – just one example of the myriad community events born from the creative ethos that the project has stimulated.

The Mural Trail is chiefly concentrated near the seafront, where two powerful and poignant sculptural monuments also catch the eye. The focus of the civic square is a war memorial dating from 1922 featuring a characterful statue of a lone soldier by William Birnie Rhind, who probably used one of his studio assistants as the model. Nearby is a boldly eloquent abstract bronze, commissioned from the Borders-based Leslie Chorley as an elegy for Prestonpans' lost industries, and erected in 1968 as part of the Scottish Arts Council's Public Sculpture Scheme.

Address The Mural Trail begins at the Prestoungrange Gothenburg, 227 High Street, Prestonpans, EH32 9BE; see www.prestoungrange.org for a map. *Witch!* is in Cuthill Park, and the Leslie Chorley sculpture is in a park on the High Street opposite Mill Wynd | Getting there Bus 26 or X26 to Prestonpans (Ox Walk) | Tip Popularly known as The Goth, the Prestoungrange Gothenburg pub is an Arts and Crafts gem, enhanced by mural interventions of a more recent date. First opened in 1908 as the Trust Tavern, it was one of dozens of pubs in the Lothians established according to 'Gothenburg Principles', which dictate that a high proportion of the profits should be returned to the community.

43 Preston Tower

Quirky medieval high-rise with glorious garden

The tall, self-contained strongholds that we call tower houses were a prominent feature of the late medieval Scottish landscape. Unmissable statements of power and prestige, they remained the nobility's preferred style of castle for around 300 years, evolving from straightforward rectangular blocks of around four storeys into an impressive range of shapes and sizes. But of all the variants that are still standing today, none is quite so quirky as Preston Tower.

Though long an empty ruin, the tower has recently benefitted from major refurbishment, which has restored public access to the interior. Standing aloof in the corner of a peaceful walled garden, it's an unexpectedly magisterial sight to come upon in Prestonpans' southern suburbs – a reminder of the time when this land was at the heart of the old community of Preston, before the focus shifted to the coastal salt pans.

Preston Tower was built by Sir Robert Hamilton when he inherited the barony in the 1460s. His residence had three storeys, plus an unusual mezzanine level, with a first-floor doorway to the living quarters reached by an external, removable wooden staircase – an important security measure to complement its six-foot-thick walls. Some 160 years later, when the need for defensive measures was less pressing, his ancestor Sir John decided to build a modern extension. But rather than adding a new wing he took the surprising step of expanding the property upwards, adding two more storeys in a lighter style, with fashionable Renaissance decoration.

Another attractive 17th-century structure is the newly restored doocot at the foot of the garden, where pigeons were kept for the laird's table. The garden itself, created in the 1980s in historical style, is an idyllic green space with much to explore and enjoy, particularly in the early summer when the glorious laburnum arch is in full bloom.

Address Cross Cottages, Prestonpans, EH32 9EJ, +44 (0)1620 827827 | Getting there
Bus 26, 111/A, 124 or 125 to Preston Road (Health Centre) | Hours Tower interior: see
www.facebook.com/FriendsOfPrestonTower; exterior and garden: unrestricted | Tip Five
minutes' walk away, Stone Fired is a popular artisan pizza place near the railway station,
serving Neapolitan-style pizzas as well as traditional Italian pasta dishes; takeaway and
home delivery only.

44 The Gegan

A secret haven – and some dangerous neighbours

Of all the glorious strands that grace East Lothian's coastline, the secluded beach at Seacliff is perhaps the most enchanting. Along with half a mile of empty golden sands and a breathtaking outlook, it boasts a delightful secret: hidden in a massive outcrop of rippled red sandstone, known as the Gegan, is a tiny harbour, thought to be the smallest in Britain.

Created in 1890 for local laird Andrew Laidlay, it was cut out of the living rock by the power of steam and compressed air. Though its entrance is less than 10 feet wide, with access from the sea by a narrow natural channel through the rocks, this little haven was once busy with flat-bottomed 'coble' fishing boats, working stake nets for salmon off the nearby River Tyne. Today, it's mainly used for diving practice – at high tide, it has a depth of around 20 feet.

Though it now seems so remote, Seacliff and its rugged surroundings have a long and at times dramatic history. The name 'Gegan' means Churchman's Rock, a homage to St Baldred, the much-mythologised missionary to the Lothians, who may have lived in a nearby cave at some time in the 8th century. We do know for sure that the Gegan was settled at least 600 years before that, thanks to finds including Roman pottery unearthed by Andrew's father J. W. Laidlay, an antiquarian who bought the Seacliff estate and its Scots-Baronial mansion after making his fortune as an indigo manufacturer in India. The grand house is now a melancholy shell, gutted in 1907 by a tragic fire that took Andrew's life.

Gloomier still is the story of a notorious gang, the Pagans of Scoughall, who on storm-torn nights used lanterns to lure ships on to Great Car, a jagged reef to the east of the bay, before plundering the wreckage. Robert Louis Stevenson, a regular visitor to the area, found inspiration for his late novel *The Wrecker* in local tales of their misdeeds.

Address Seacliff, EH39 5PP | Getting there Bus 120 to Auldhame Farm, then follow private road to beach car park (0.7 mile). Drivers should note that this road has a coin-operated barrier. The Gegan is at the west end of the beach. | Tip Fabulous views of Tantallon can be enjoyed from the Gegan. Look out also for the ruined Auldhame Castle, on a headland to the west of the beach, and the gaunt remains of Seacliff House, hidden in trees a little way inland, to the south.

45 Torness Power Station

Get to the core of the energy question

It's a fair bet that 'tour a nuclear power plant' doesn't feature on most people's bucket list – but perhaps it ought to. The thought probably conjures up alarming images gleaned from old James Bond films. But if you're looking for an out-of-the-ordinary, eye-opening experience that you won't forget in a hurry, the chance to see for yourself how one of these technological marvels *really* operates should tick all the boxes.

Torness power station is a rare bird in the nuclear community – an advanced gas-cooled reactor, the last of its kind to be commissioned in the UK. It's a prominent East Lothian landmark, on an isolated coastal site by the A1; most people who glimpse it from afar assume that visitors are not welcome, but it has in fact offered free public tours since its early days. It was a controversial project when first proposed in the 1970s, but although nuclear energy remains a divisive issue, most opinions locally, where it's a valued source of skilled employment, have mellowed considerably in the decades since.

Tours begin at the Visitor Centre, where a well-mounted exhibition provides a useful introduction to a mind-boggling subject. Friendly, informative guides then lead you through the vast, labyrinthine complex to a series of viewing galleries, keeping up an admirably clear commentary filled with unexpected insights as you gaze down in awe on the turbine hall, reactor building and surprisingly retro-style control room.

Since it began operating in 1988, Torness has generated enough electricity to power every home in Scotland for 29 years, but it's now coming to the end of its working life, and is scheduled to close in 2028. Get in there while you can: as we all wake up to the enormity of the global energy crisis, it surely makes sense to learn the facts about the facilities that provide the world's second-largest source of low-carbon power.

Address Torness, EH42 1QS, +44 (0)1368 873909, www.edfenergy.com/energy/
power-stations/torness | Getting there Off A 1, six miles south of Dunbar; bus 253
from Dunbar to Crowhill and a 30-minute walk | Hours Visitor Centre Mon–Thu
9am–4pm; site tours (1.5 hours) must be booked at least three weeks in advance; email
tornessvisitorcentre@edf-energy.com for full details | Tip Just along the coast to the west
at Skateraw beach is a mysterious-looking rectangular stone building, 20 feet high, with
intriguing round-arched openings. This is a 19th-century limekiln, a relic of an important
local industry. Fired by coal landed at the adjacent harbour, its purpose was to burn
limestone to create quicklime, chiefly for use as fertilizer by farmers.

46 Castlelaw Hill Fort
A secret passage to the Iron Age

The Pentland Hills have seen an awful lot of history, though the traces left by the ancient generations whose lives unfolded on its uplands may seem negligible and disappointing to the uninitiated. One notable exception can be found at Castlelaw, an Iron Age hill fort prominently situated on a lower spur of the heights of Castle Knowe, nearly 1,000 feet above sea level and commanding a wide sweep of land across the Lothians and beyond.

Dating from around 500 B.C. and occupied for several centuries, this wasn't a fort in the military sense but an enclosed village, home to a farming community who protected their territory with rings of earthwork banks and ditches – still clearly visible, though best appreciated from higher up the hillside. Similar elements can be seen at other sites in the area, but what gives Castlelaw its particular fascination is the mysterious subterranean structure hidden beneath the turf. Built into one of the ditches is a curved, stone-lined passageway some 65 feet long, with a large beehive-shaped chamber off to one side. Known as a souterrain (French for 'underground'), it's thought to date from the first century A.D., one of the last periods when people lived here. After its excavation in the 1930s, it was given a concrete roof and skylights, making it easier to explore though detracting somewhat from the atmosphere.

Souterrains have been found in many parts of Scotland as well as in Brittany, Cornwall and Ireland, but despite considerable speculation there is no consensus as to their purpose. Though always associated with settlements, they're not living spaces, or indeed tombs, and the fact that they only have a single entrance makes it unlikely that they were hiding places. Some archaeologists claim that they were simply storage areas, used for grain or dairy produce, but a more compelling theory is that they were designed for rituals or ceremonies – rites of passage, perhaps, figuratively as well as literally.

Address Castle Knowe, Pentland Hills, nearest postcode EH26 0PD,
www.historicenvironment.scot/visit-a-place/places/castlelaw-hill-fort | Getting there
Bus 101, 101A, 102 to Flotterstone Inn and one-mile uphill walk on minor road (signposted),
then a short, steep path | Hours Daily Apr–Sept, 9.30am–5.30pm, Oct–Mar 10am–4pm
(last entry 3.30pm) | Tip Just beyond the bus stop, the Flotterstone Inn is a historic roadside
pub and restaurant with a beer garden, popular with walkers. A path behind it leads to the
Pentland Hills Information Centre, which has maps of local walking routes including the
easy and rewarding track up to Glencorse Reservoir.

47__Cousland Smiddy
A community forging solid links with its past

Watching a blacksmith fashioning metal is spellbinding; there's a mysterious alchemy to this age-old craft that makes it easy to understand why its earliest practitioners were revered in ancient cultures as gods and magicians. By the Middle Ages, the smith had become an essential part of every community, making and repairing the tools and utensils necessary for daily life, and shoeing the horses that later powered both agriculture and industry. The blacksmith's shop was also the focus of village social life, a gathering place where local folk would meet to chat about the issues of the day. On summer evenings games of quoits were often played, using horseshoes, and until well into the last century the searing glow of the forge, clang and sparks of hammer on anvil, and the hiss of hot metal thrust into cooling water, were sights and sounds familiar to all.

It seems miraculous to be able to enter this lost world today – and in a village just seven miles from Edinburgh. The astonishingly intact smiddy at Cousland has been in continuous use for over 300 years, thanks latterly to the sterling work of a local trust in maintaining it as both a community hub and a living heritage amenity unique in Scotland. The project began in 1986, when fourth-generation blacksmith Kit Sked announced he was retiring; resourceful villagers determined not only to preserve the historic smiddy and its contents – a copious range of equipment and tools, including 71 pairs of tongs – but to keep it in use by leasing it as a working concern. The latest resident smith is Sean Broadfoot, a master of the skilful art of farriery, or the shoeing of horses, who can be seen on open days forging metal into the familiar U-shape, and even, if you're very lucky, fitting out a four-legged client.

Besides the characterful smiddy itself, with its pantiled roof and equine-friendly entrance, the complex comprises a paddock, orchard and allotments, plus the restored smith's cottage, which houses a local history archive and displays – all well worth exploring.

Address 31 Hadfast Road, Cousland, EH22 2NZ, +44 (0)131 663 8118,
www.couslandsmiddy.co.uk | **Getting there** Off A6094, 3 miles east of Dalkeith |
Hours Various Sats from mid-Apr to mid-Oct, 10am–1pm, plus Doors Open Day in
Sept, or by appointment; see website | **Tip** A little way north of Cousland is Carberry Hill,
the site on 15 June 1567 of a fateful encounter between forces loyal to Mary, Queen of
Scots and a band of rebel lords. Mary surrendered after a stand-off and the escape of her
husband Bothwell; she was then imprisoned, forced to abdicate and ultimately executed.
A monument marks the place where the 24-year-old queen spent her last hours of freedom.

48 Dalkeith Country Park

Culture, adventure, ancient oaks and shopping

Walk to the quieter northern end of Dalkeith's busy High Street and you'll soon see a gateway leading into a stretch of peaceful parkland. It's so near the town centre that you'd expect this to be a modest municipal affair, but what you'll actually find is an expansive country estate with 1,000 acres of scenic spendour and historic interest to explore, plus added attractions from adventure parks to quality retail and food outlets. Meandering through it all are twin rivers, the North and South Esk, which come together in a confluence known poetically as the Meeting of the Waters.

The landscape as we see it today was created by successive generations of the Buccleuch family as a setting for Dalkeith Palace, one of Scotland's earliest grand classical mansions, completed in 1711 for Anne, the first Duchess, and incorporating an older castle. It's had a chequered history for the past century or so, including a recent spell as an outpost of an American university, but has now reopened to the public, with a programme of exhibitions and tours in the summer. Other architectural gems include the lofty Montagu Bridge, designed by Robert Adam, a stable block by his father William (now attractively renovated as Restoration Yard store and café) and a flamboyantly ornate 12-sided conservatory, built in the 1830s for a failed experiment to grow oranges. For family fun and thrills, there are two woodland adventure parks featuring turreted treehouses, aerial walkways and zip wires, open to adults as well as children.

Waymarked trails at levels from easy to moderately challenging take you through the natural glories of the wider park, whose woodlands shelter a variety of bird, mammal and insect life. There are snowdrops to be admired in February, bluebells in May, and oak trees of venerable antiquity, seeded from the native Caledonian forest and enchanting at any season.

Address Dalkeith, EH22 1ST, www.dalkeithcountrypark.co.uk | **Getting there** Bus 3, 46, 48, 51, 139, 140, 141 or X33 to Dalkeith town centre; entrance for pedestrians is the Town Gate (EH22 2NA) at the north end of the High Street. Note that drivers should use King's Gate, EH22 1ST | **Hours** Daily 7am–7pm, Restoration Yard 10am–5pm; Fort Douglas and Go Ape adventure parks 10am–1pm & 2–5pm (booking advisable) | **Tip** On the southern edge of the town, Newbattle Abbey is a historic stately home incorporating parts of a 12th-century monastery, with 125-acre grounds featuring a formal Italian garden. The home of an adult educational college for many decades, it's also a venue for conferences, weddings and other occasions. Contact the college to enquire about tours (www.newbattleabbey.com).

49_Dalkeith Museum

Potent memories of life in a proud community

Dalkeith's Corn Exchange is a magnificent affair, built in 1853 in confident 'Jacobethan' style to house its grain market, the largest in Scotland. Crowned by a splendid hammerbeam roof, the capacious hall went on to play a central role in the life of the community for over a century, as a venue for events of all kinds, before changing fortunes led to a long period of neglect and eventual abandonment. In 2016, however, it reopened at last, elegantly restored for a new dual use: a housing association occupies the main space, while an easily-missed section to the rear has been converted into a fitting home for the town museum.

It's a relatively small space, but it packs in a huge amount, with themed displays on the heritage of the area that cover everything from agriculture, industry, domestic life and leisure to transport, crime and war. Your attention is immediately drawn to a proud figure in ceremonial scarlet jacket and tartan trews – a lieutenant of the 8th Battalion Royal Scots, a local territorial force who were among the first British troops to be deployed to France in World War I. There's a fascinating display exploring Dalkeith's role in a famous Victorian criminal investigation, when two accomplices of John Henry Greatrex, a prolific Glasgow-based banknote forger, were arrested by the town's police after an ill-advised spending spree in the High Street. And the oldest exhibit is a real curiosity – a striking life-sized stone sculpture of a human head, thought to be related to the vast Roman fort that stood nearby in the A.D. 70s.

The Corn Exchange has its own rich history, including a spell as an Edwardian roller-skating rink. It later housed a ballroom, the fondly remembered Empress, which in 1947 became the first dance hall in Scotland licensed to open on Sundays. So popular were its shindigs that special late buses were laid on for the many hundreds of young folk who came down from Edinburgh for the evening.

Address 61 St Andrew Street, Dalkeith, EH22 1BP, +44 (0)131 663 4683,
www.dalkeithhistorysociety.co.uk/dalkeith-museum | Getting there Bus 3, 46, 48, 51,
139, 140, 141 or X33 to Dalkeith town centre. Note that there is no access to the
museum from the main (High Street) entrance to the Corn Exchange | Hours Tue–Thu
10.30am–3.30pm | Tip The museum is run by the dedicated volunteers of Dalkeith History
Society, who also organise a varied programme of events. In addition to an excellent series of
monthly talks, there are guided evening walking tours of the town where you are invited to
explore its 'dark and deadly' secrets (not suitable for children).

50 Dalkeith Water Tower

A refreshing taste of the high life

Historic towers have an irresistibly romantic appeal, no matter how utilitarian their original function. Dalkeith boasts a fine example in the shape of an 80-foot-tall octagonal pagoda, built in the Victorian era to house an elevated tank for the municipal water supply, and still standing proud nearly 150 years later. With its decorative polychrome brickwork and timber-clad crown, it remained a cherished local landmark long after it fell into disuse and, thanks to a remarkable conversion over four decades ago, is now enjoying a second life as a holiday home.

Dalkeith's very first Town Council was elected in 1878, making it the last place in Scotland to reap the benefits of 19th-century local government reform. Their most pressing priority was the improvement of the public drinking water supply, and this was achieved the following year with the completion of the tower. At the top was a wrought-iron tank with a capacity of around 18,000 gallons; water was pumped up to it from sources including a nearby artesian well, and distributed by gravity to a piped infrastructure. As a neat corollary, the site of the old reservoir was soon occupied by the brand new Council Chambers, in fitting Scots-Baronial style.

The water tower quietly served its purpose until the 1950s, when it was rendered redundant. Thankfully, however, it did not meet the crushing fate that befell so many icons of Victorian industrial architecture in those days, and in 1976 it was Grade B listed. Plans to convert it into a camera obscura came to nothing, but in 1988 its future was secured when it was bought by architect Gerry Goldwyre and his wife Susan. They carefully transformed it into an exceptional seven-floor family home, now let out as holiday accommodation. One particularly inspired idea was the addition of a wrap-around balcony, which offers unbeatable views over Midlothian and beyond.

Address Cemetery Road, Dalkcith, EH22 3DL, www.facebook.com/dalkeithwatertower | **Getting there** Bus 3, 48, 49, 51, 140 or 141 to Dalkeith town centre | **Hours** For short-term lets (minimum three nights, sleeps up to four) see www.airbnb.co.uk; otherwise viewable from the outside only | **Tip** Despite the blight of a 1960s brutalist development that took the heart out of the town, Dalkeith still has many buildings of historic interest, which are highlighted on a useful Town Trail information board in the square on the High Street. Look out for the solemn Watch Tower (also octagonal) in Old Edinburgh Road Cemetery, built in 1827 to enable a night-time lookout for grave robbers.

51__Old Pentland Kirkyard
The grave history of a peaceful knoll

The scattered community of Damhead occupies a green pocket on the edge of the Pentlands that feels surprisingly secluded from the traffic-heavy roads and development on its fringes. In the midst of this rural peace, a yew-clad knoll hides a further surprise – an abandoned graveyard, restored thanks to local initiative, with links to two darkly momentous chapters in Scotland's past.

There's no trace of the 13th-century parish church that once stood here, and an austere mausoleum now dominates the site. Though to some eyes it may resemble a modern domestic garage, it was designed in 1839 by eminent Neoclassicist Thomas Hamilton, for local lairds the Gibsones. There are also several 17th- and 18th-century headstones, carved with evocative imagery. But the most significant graves here have no markers, for they contain the remains of a group of Covenanters – religious dissenters, killed by government troops at the Battle of Rullion Green on 28 November 1666. This was the culmination of the Pentland Rising, when outlawed Presbyterians, persecuted for their refusal to recognise the king as the head of the church, raised a volunteer army to confront their oppressors. The untrained fighters were defeated with the loss of an estimated 60 men; many others who fled were captured and brutally executed.

Three quarters of a century later, Old Pentland gained a grim notoriety after the arrest of an Edinburgh gardener, on his way to the city's Medical School with a child's body stolen from the cemetery. This was during an epidemic of grave robbing in and around the capital that led to rioting, and soon necessitated the construction of the watch house at the entrance, where relatives could keep vigil over new burials. Two 13th-century stones carved with symbols sacred to the Knights Templar are housed inside. Also from this site is a vivid 17th-century carving, now in the crypt of Rosslyn Chapel, with the apt subject of Death as the King of Terrors.

Address Pentland Road, Old Pentland, EH10 7EA | Getting there Bus 47, 47B, X37 or X62 to Straiton Road (Asda) and a 10-minute walk along Pentland Road | Tip The site of the Battle of Rullion Green is marked by a memorial dating from 1738, in woodland to the west of the A702, south-west of Flotterstone. A much grander monument – the Colinton Column – was erected c. 1886 outside Dreghorn Barracks on Redford Road, Edinburgh, and commemorates four historical military campaigns, including that of the Pentland Rising.

52 Mavisbank
New life for a fragile classical ideal

It seems barely credible today that the elegant Georgian terraces of Edinburgh's New Town came close to wholesale demolition back in the novelty-seeking 1960s. But the story of Mavisbank House, a ruinous 18th-century villa seven miles south of the capital, serves as a salutary reminder that battles are still being fought to preserve this country's most significant historic buildings. The Neoclassical gem – which predates the New Town by more than 40 years – was gutted by fire in 1973 and left a derelict shell, with the threat of the wrecker's ball ever present as its condition grew increasingly parlous. It was only in May 2024, after decades of tireless campaigning by concerned locals and architectural historians, that news finally came of a major grant from the National Heritage Memorial Fund, which will fund its restoration by the Landmark Trust.

Mavisbank was designed in 1723 by the celebrated architect William Adam, working closely with his client, the multi-talented Sir John Clerk of Penicuik, a prominent figure in the Scottish Enlightenment. Clerk's innovative vision was to bring the ideals of the Ancient Roman villa to his homeland, siting his classically inspired country retreat within a picturesque, landscaped park; one admiring visitor declared that the whole ensemble seemed like a valley near Tivoli rather than Edinburgh. It was a radical rethink of the concept of a noble residence, which proved hugely influential on the course of Scottish architecture.

The house's later history included a spell as a pioneering mental hospital, before its purchase in the 1950s by a philistine owner whose wilful neglect of the property extended beyond the grave, ensuring legal complications that blocked all attempts to save it. Thankfully, these have at last been resolved, and Mavisbank will now be brought back to life for future generations to enjoy.

Address Mavisbank Estate, Polton, Lasswade, EH18 1HY | **Getting there** For pedestrian access to the grounds, bus 31 or 49 to Polton Road West or 31 or 140 to Kevock Road | **Hours** Grounds: unrestricted; house: currently viewable from the outside only, behind security fence. Once the building has been stabilised, The Landmark Trust plans to offer public tours behind the scenes to observe its restoration. In the longer term it will be let out as holiday accommodation, with regular free open days. | **Tip** The Mavisbank Estate is home to many ancient trees, including a remarkable rowan known as the Portal Tree, which has grown in the shape of an inverted U, forming an archway. In 2022 it was shortlisted as the Woodland Trust's Tree of the Year and won second place.

53 _ The Secret Herb Garden

Glasshouse dining and handcrafted gin

It took a rare vision to create the phenomenon that is the Secret Herb Garden. A unique combination of botanical oasis, glasshouse bistro and gin distillery, the garden had its genesis in 2012 when herbologist Hamish Martin, a former wine merchant, chanced upon a derelict seven-acre agricultural holding at the foot of Pentland Hills, in an area then best known for the mammoth Ikea store along the road. He and his wife Liberty spent the next three years living in a caravan on the site with their young family while they developed the land and its ruined glasshouses into an engagingly quirky herb nursery with a café and shop.

Within a few years of its opening in 2014, the venture had grown to encompass a beehouse, rose garden and event space. The expansion into gin production in 2017, which made it the UK's only botanical garden with its own distillery, originally came about as an insurance measure, after a long dispute with the local council over the use of the garden as a wedding venue. But it turned out to be an inspired move, which saw visitor numbers triple within two years.

Now under new ownership, the garden continues to thrive, with some 600 different plants grown according to the philosophy of permaculture, and enhanced features such as an educational juniper woodland. Its café-bistro offers the delightful opportunity to enjoy breakfast, lunch or afternoon tea within a glasshouse filled with vines and lush greenery, plus, once a month, a romantic dinner to coincide with each full moon.

The gins, all crafted on site from hand-harvested botanicals, come in a range of subtle flavours including 'Wild', which uses plants often dismissed as weeds, as well as Elderflower and Jasmine, Rose, Lavender, and Lemon Verbena. New eco-friendly packaging includes bespoke bottles featuring the garden's signature bee logo on the stopper, in tribute to the hard-working insects that have been part of its life and ethos from the start.

Address 32A Old Pentland Road, Lothianburn, EH10 7EA, +44 (0)131 374 5605 (café),
+44 (0)131 285 6833 (distillery) | Getting there Bus 15 to Old Pentland Road and a
10-minute walk along Burnside Road, or 47, 47B, X37 or X62 to Asda Straiton and a
15-minute walk along Pentland Road | Hours Garden and café-bistro: daily 10am–4pm;
see www.secretherbgarden-cafebistro.co.uk for dates of Full Moon Dinners. Gin tours and
tastings: Thu–Sun, see www.secretgardendistillery.co.uk for times and bookings | Tip The
picturesque hamlet of Swanston, a rarity in Scotland with its thatched cottages and village
green, stands less than two miles north west, at the gateway to the Pentland Hills Regional
Park. Nearby Swanston Farm has a popular family restaurant with Highland cows grazing
in the vicinity.

54 Huly Hill

Speeding through time

Amid the soulless sprawl of asphalt and concrete at the limits of Edinburgh's western hinterland is a pleasant pocket of green space, featuring three big chunks of stone flanking a low grassy knoll. It's an odd public park, in a curious location – next to Scotland's busiest motorway interchange, alarmingly close to the main runway of its biggest airport and hemmed in by a slew of high-end car dealerships. But this oasis is far more than a recreation ground for local dog walkers: it is in fact the remnant of a prehistoric gathering place, a ceremonial site whose construction must have involved a massive community effort.

Neatly ringed by a modern retaining wall, the mound known as Huly Hill is a Bronze Age grave monument, marking the burial around 2,500 B.C. of one or more powerful individuals. The three intriguingly shaped monoliths that surround it are the remains of a stone circle, of similar date; a fourth outlier is marooned beyond the roundabout. The original appearance of these monuments is impossible to imagine now, with the cluttered horizon dominated by dispiriting features such as the golden arches of a certain fast-food purveyor. But they still possess a timeless power and serenity that somehow isn't dispelled by the fleeting roar of massive jetliners directly overhead.

The continuing significance of this place in later antiquity was confirmed in 2001, when an archaeological excavation on a nearby building site uncovered a high-status burial from the 5th century B.C. It contained the remains of a chariot, a state-of-the-art vehicle built for speed – and an apposite reminder that fast, stylish travel has been a human preoccupation for millennia. Though no trace of the charioteer survives, some comparable British Iron Age graves contain the remains of female drivers – which raises the interesting possibility that this Celtic boy racer was actually a woman.

Address Bridge Street, Newbridge, EH28 8SH, immediately west of the Newbridge Roundabout (M8/M9 interchange) | Getting there Bus 18, X 18, X 24, X 25, X 38, X 51 or 63 to Newbridge | Tip The remains of the Newbridge Chariot are in the collections of the National Museums of Scotland in Edinburgh, along with a superb full-scale reconstruction of the extraordinary find, made in 2007. Images can be seen on the NMS website together with a fascinating video describing its creation.

55__The Dean Tavern

Your friendly neighbourhood Goth

A bright and welcoming hostelry in genteel Arts-and-Crafts style might seem an unexpected sight in a former mining village, but then the Dean Tavern is not your average Scottish howff. Those in the know should get a hint from the font in which its name is spelled out on the façade: this fine Edwardian-era local is a 'Goth', a rare survivor of a social experiment to control heavy drinking that bene-fitted many communities across the Scottish industrial heartland in the late 19th and early 20th centuries.

The nickname has nothing to do with the youth subculture, or indeed medieval churches: it's a contraction of Gothenburg, the Swedish city where the scheme originated in 1865. Its aim was to discourage 'immoderation' while promoting healthier pursuits, by putting licensed premises in the hands of trustees who used the profits to pay for public recreational and cultural amenities. The Gothenburg System was soon taken up by reformers in Scotland, particularly in mining villages, as the model for a new kind of pub – well-managed, respectable establishments, often incorporating res-taurants, which funded resources such as libraries, parks and sports facilities. Interestingly, the architectural style most commonly cho-sen was quite alien to the Scottish tradition, with half-timbered gables and cottagey elements that would look more at home in southern England.

Initially established in 1899 for the miners from the local colliery, the Dean Tavern is the only remaining Gothenburg pub in Scotland still run according to the original principles. It's a real community local, highly rated for its good-value food and drink, family- and dog-friendly and with regular live entertainment. Among the initiatives that it currently supports are the local football team, a silver band, Scotland's second-largest pétanque club and Newtongrange's annual Gala Day, proudly going strong since 1913.

Address 80 Main Street, Newtongrange,EH22 4NA, +44 (0)131 663 2419, www.deantavern.co.uk | **Getting there** Train to Newtongrange and a 10-minute walk; bus 29, 48, X95 or 339 to the door | **Hours** Mon–Thu & Sun 11am–11pm, Fri & Sat 11am–midnight | **Tip** Newtongrange is home to a five-star visitor attraction, the National Mining Museum, established in 1982 to preserve the impressive buildings and pit-head machinery of the former Lady Victoria Colliery, Scotland's first super-pit. Guided tours are led by ex-miners with fascinating personal anecdotes to relate about life at the coal face.

56 Seilich Botanicals
Wild nature distilled with care

Wildflower meadows are a rare sight today – 97 per cent of the species-rich grasslands that flourished across Britain a century ago have gone. But there's one pocket of the Lothian countryside where this grievous destruction is being reversed: a green oasis restored to floral wildness by Dr Sally Gouldstone, founder of the award-winning Seilich Botanicals. Seilich is a natural skincare company with a genuinely nature-friendly ethos. Its products are based on wild flowers hand-harvested in a sustainable way, and the profits fund the expansion of the meadow, a highly effective carbon sink as well as a welcoming habitat for wildlife that buzzes with biodiversity.

Sally founded Seilich – Gaelic for Willow, her daughter's name – in 2019, after a 20-year career as a research botanist and conservationist. Her inspiration for the business came from a growing indignation at the beauty industry's cynical marketing of products that are claimed to be eco-friendly but that are actually damaging the environment in multiple ways. Renting a couple of acres of former arable land on the Preston Hall estate, she seeded the worn-out soil with a mix of native plants known for their therapeutic properties, such as wild carrot, yarrow, comfrey, red clover and plantain. As the meadow matured, Sally secured a workshop on the same site, bought a traditional copper still and began extracting the potent essential oils and hydrosols that are the key constituents of Seilich's products. Meanwhile, she started to spread the word, teaching local community groups how to create their own meadows and running cosmetics-making workshops.

As the business has grown, so has Sally's meadow – to the size of four and a half football pitches. In summer it hosts a range of events where you can immerse yourself in activities from yoga to sketching, while savouring the uplifting and restorative power of nature.

Address Unit 1, Rosemains Steading, Pathhead, EH37 5UQ, +44 (0)7776 812513, www.seilich.co.uk | Getting there Off B 6367, 1.5 miles north-east of Pathhead | Hours See website for programme of workshops and meadow experiences | Tip Nearby Preston Hall has an impressive two-acre walled garden with attractive twin gazebos, dating from c. 1806 and recently rescued from overgrown dereliction. There are regular summer open days (with pop-up café) and the space can also be hired for weddings and functions.

57 __ The Papermaking Museum

Rags, riches and stowaway tortoises

Paper was one of the most significant inventions in history, and despite our increasing thralldom to digital media and plastic, we still couldn't function without it. For nearly 300 years Penicuik was a major centre for the manufacture of this wondrous material – there were once signs on its approach roads proclaiming it as The Papermaking Town – and though the last mill closed in 2004, the community now celebrates its heritage in the only museum in Scotland devoted to the subject.

It was a woman who brought the craft to Penicuik – the redoutable Agnes Campbell, who had inherited her late husband's role as Royal Printer. In 1709 she established the first paper mill on the River Esk, which provided the copious quantities of water necessary for processing the raw material of linen and cotton rags. The business thrived, and in 1779 the Cowan family, who became a major force for social reform in the town, took over the site and renamed it Valleyfield. They soon introduced modern technology such as the Hollander rag-beating engine, and Penicuik grew so prosperous from papermaking that in 1793 it was noted that the expensive commodity of tea was 'frequently drunk even among the lowest of people'. By 1836 the Valleyfield mills were producing 20 miles of paper per day. Before long, new raw materials had to be found to cope with demand, most notably esparto grass from North Africa, which made a high-quality, much sought-after product. One unexpected result was the accidental importation of tortoises hibernating in the bales, which were often adopted by workers as family pets.

The full, fascinating story is told with the aid of enthusiastic volunteer guides, who will also help you make your own sheet of paper as a souvenir. After your tour, be sure to pop into the Pen-y-Coe Press, a traditional printer's and stationery shop next door that operates as a living museum.

Address 7 Bridge Street, Penicuik, EH26 8LL, +44 (0)1968 673767, www.penicuikcdt.co.uk | **Getting there** Bus 37, 47, 101, 102, 140 or X62 to Penicuik town centre | **Hours** Apr–Nov, Sat 1–3.30pm, or by appointment; Pen-y-Coe Press, Tue–Sat 10am–4pm | **Tip** Penicuik Storehouse is an excellent community venture in the town centre, with a cosy café and a well-stocked shop selling organic vegetables, fruit and groceries, household products and locally made craft items.

58 Penicuik Estate

Glorious creation of the clever Clerks

On the doorstep of Penicuik, just off the busy road that rumbles down from Edinburgh, is a pathway leading to a realm of soul-refreshing peace. One of Scotland's greatest historic landscaped parks, it was created by a remarkable dynasty, the Clerks of Penicuik, and is now freely open to all.

At the heart of the estate is a palatial Neoclassical mansion, built in the 1760s by the 3rd baronet, Sir James Clerk, an avid patron of the arts. Famous figures of the Scottish Enlightenment once communed here, while admiring his classical statuary and paintings by the eccentric Alexander Runciman. Though still a majestic sight, the house has stood roofless and gutted since a devastating fire in 1899. Thereafter, the Clerks made their home in Sir James' stable block – a stylish curiosity, crowned by an elegant spire and a domed doocot (pigeon house) modelled on Arthur's O'on, a strange igloo-shaped Roman temple near Falkirk that was demolished in 1743.

But it is James' father, the polymath 2nd baronet Sir John, that we must thank for the glorious 500-hectare parkland, which has survived largely unaltered since its creation in the early 18th century. Besides his skills in fields from politics to musical composition, Sir John was a pioneer of landscape design, and his inspired transformation of the estate according to the poetic and pastoral ideals of classical literature proved hugely influential.

Today there are over 12 miles of trails, taking in enchanting woodlands and a perfectly placed ornamental lake, as well as the River North Esk, which bisects the estate. Sight lines lead the eye to a series of dramatic landmarks, among them an obelisk dedicated to poet Allan Ramsay and the castellated Flag Tower. This monument had a practical purpose – it's another doocot, with 1,356 nestboxes. It seems those enlightened folk just couldn't get enough pigeon meat.

Address Penicuik Estate, EH26 9JE, www.penicuikestate.com | Getting there Bus 37, 47, 101, 102, 140 or X62 to Penicuik town centre, then walk down Bridge Street and turn right into Cairnbank Road, which leads to a footpath into the park | Hours Accessible 24 hours | Tip Various properties on the estate are available to rent, including restored cottages and newly built luxury cabins in the woods. New Penicuik House itself (the former stable block) will shortly be launched as a 15-bedroom exclusive-use venue (see website for details).

59__Tormain Hill

Mesmerising ancient geometry on the rocks

The low but prominent wooded ridge of Tormain rises just south of the quiet village of Ratho. It's such a short and gentle climb, up a well-worn path on the western slope, that you hardly feel deserving of the rewards in store as you approach the summit. Not only are the all-round views from the fringes of the woodland unexpectedly far-reaching and spectacular, the atmosphere of soothing tranquillity is palpable. The teeming clamour of motorways, railways and airport just down the road seems worlds away, a sensation that intensifies if you adjust your focus to your immediate surroundings.

Half-hidden in the turf is a scattering of whinstone outcrops decorated with enigmatic carvings dating from around 5,000 years ago, the time of Scotland's earliest farmers. Known as cup and ring marks, these curvilinear grooves and hollows were incised into the hard bedrock using stone tools – a lengthy, laborious process. At least seven sets of markings have been uncovered here, though not all are visible today. A massive boulder carved with a line of cup marks once stood in a nearby field; dubbed the Witches' Stone, it was broken up in the early 20th century, perhaps due to superstition.

Rock art of this kind has been recorded in more than 3,000 locations in Scotland, and Tormain is just one of a cluster of upland sites around the Pentland Hills and present-day Edinburgh where it occurs. The purpose of the ornamentation has long been debated – in the 1970s, one author listed over 100 diverse theories, ranging from star maps to musical notation to sacrificial altars. More prosaic recent speculation suggests they could be practice tablets for student stoneworkers, or boundary markers for seasonal animal grazing. We'll never know the truth, but it's impossible not to muse about these haunting relics of a vanished world as you gaze out at the much-altered panorama.

Address Tormain, near Ratho, EH27 8BB | Getting there Bus 20 to Ratho (Wilkieston Road) and a 15-minute walk. Follow road out of the village, then cross to join signposted footpath. The cup-and-ring marked stones are near the summit; look for the stone by the path carved with an arrow (a 19th-century triangulation point), which helpfully points towards the most striking one (illustrated) | Hours Always accessible; best viewed in early morning or late afternoon on a bright day in winter or spring, when the sun is low | Tip Less than two miles south, on the A71 near the junction with Linburn Road, stands a splendid but derelict gateway adorned with elegant ironwork. Originally erected in 1692, it's part of the scant remains of one of Scotland's finest Renaissance mansions, Hatton House.

60 The Gunpowder Mills

The explosive past of a picturesque dell

For centuries, the dramatic wooded gorge of Roslin Glen has drawn visitors seeking rugged scenery enhanced by romantic historical lore. With glorious walks along the meandering North Esk, overlooked by two clifftop castles – plus the stellar Rosslyn Chapel – it's been a huge source of inspiration for writers, most influentially Sir Walter Scott, who brought the area to mass attention in his 1805 epic *The Lay of the Last Minstrel*. But just as the glen and its monuments were enjoying their first wave of literary and antiquarian tourism, a toxic and hazardous industry was taking hold a short way upstream: gunpowder manufacture.

The Roslin factory was founded in 1804, when a high demand for the 'black powder' was guaranteed, thanks to the onset of the Napoleonic Wars, as well as the growing needs of the mining and quarrying industries. The glen made an ideal site: plentiful river water was on hand to power the mills that ground the powder, and the manufacture could be carried out in widely spaced buildings, mostly recessed into the towering tree-clad rock. This minimised the effects of accidents, of which there were many, often fatal. The locale also provided alder wood for charcoal, one of just three ingredients required for the explosive mixture, the others being saltpetre, imported from India, and sulphur, from Sicily.

Though surely the epitome of all the places that ever merited the tag of 'dark satanic mills', the gunpowder factory was a valued source of local employment; it grew to become the largest complex of its kind in Scotland, remaining operational until 1954 and demolished as late as the 1970s. Most of the scant remains now lie buried in leafy tranquillity amid meadows of wild garlic, though the ruined mill near the weir is an unexpectedly picturesque sight, with the high sandstone bluff of Harecraig making a stunning backdrop across the river.

Address Roslin Glen Country Park, Roslin, EH25 9PX | **Getting there** Bus 37 or 140 to Roslin (Original Rosslyn Hotel), then a 1.2 mile walk: follow signposted footpath from Chapel Loan, via Jacob's Ladder (a 76-step stairway) to the park entrance, at a sharp bend on the B 7003. A well-made route with interpretation panels leads to the mill ruins | **Tip** Roslin's three remarkable medieval monuments have very different present-day uses: Hawthornden Castle is owned by a charitable foundation that provides retreats for creative writers (www.hawthornden.org), Roslin Castle is let as a holiday home through the Landmark Trust, and Rosslyn Chapel is a perennial magnet for *Da Vinci Code*-inspired tourists, while remaining an atmospheric place of worship.

61 Soutra Aisle

Reconstructing medicines from the mud

The stone hut that stands on the high and windy summit of Soutra seems a long way from anywhere today but, amazingly, its lonely moorland site was once a busy and important place. It lay on the ancient *Via Regia*, the Anglo-Scottish highway that followed the line of the Roman Dere Street, at a key point that formed the gateway to the Lothians, commanding a panorama that 'gives such a throb of pleasure to the heart as is not to be described', in the words of an eloquent chronicler of 1792.

But it wasn't just the breathtaking view that drew medieval travellers to stop here. The little building is in fact a fragment of the Hospital of the Holy Trinity, a vast infirmary run by an Augustinian brotherhood that operated here from the 12th to the 16th century, serving wayfarers, pilgrims, the poor and the aged. Converted into a burial vault in the 17th century, Soutra Aisle is all that remains visible; below ground, however, it's a different story. Excavations since the 1980s have yielded an astonishing cache of medical waste, human remains and plants, including the potent trio of henbane, opium poppy and hemlock, well preserved in the waterlogged clay soil. Thanks to investigations led by archaeologist Dr Brian Moffat, these have provided fascinating insights into remedies, anaesthetics and medical practices used in the Middle Ages in specialisms from dentistry to childbirth, as well as shedding light on the management of epidemics and treatment of mental illness.

It's estimated that up to 300 monks and servants once lived here, but in the 1460s a misconduct scandal led to the sacking of the Master in charge. The hospital's rich estates (their main source of income) were confiscated by the crown and transferred to a new foundation in Edinburgh. Soutra's loss was the capital's gain, for this marked the beginning of its rise as a medical centre of international renown.

Address Soutra, near Pathhead, EH37 5TF | Getting there On B 6368, 2.3 miles south of Fala village (signposted from both A 68 and A 7); Borders bus 51 to Gilston Road End and a 15-minute walk | Hours Site accessible 24 hours; open days with Dr Brian Moffat: Easter weekend, last weekend in August (Sat – Mon), 2 – 5pm and other dates (contact brianmoffat@soutraaisle.org) | Tip A section of Dere Street, the Roman road leading from York that was used by their forces on their many incursions into Scotland, can be seen a short way south-west of Soutra Aisle.

62__Abercorn Museum

Time-worn relics of a hallowed place

Shielded in seclusion amid the tall trees and high walls of the vast Hopetoun Estate, the sleepy hamlet of Abercorn was a long way off the tourist radar until the huge transatlantic success of the *Outlander* TV series. Now, the droves of die-hard fans touring its filming locations who seek out nearby Midhope Castle (the fictional Lallybroch) generally also take in 'quaint' Abercorn churchyard which, in one episode, stood in implausibly for a cemetery in the US city of Boston.

Travellers keener on authenticity should, however, linger for longer than it takes to bag a selfie, for modest Abercorn was once a place of genuine and continuing significance. The atmospheric site may have accommodated a Roman fort during the Antonine occupation, but its greatest importance, believed to date from a visit by the missionary St Ninian over 1,500 years ago, was as a focal point for the early Christian church. A monastery and bishopric recorded by Bede, the venerable chronicler, were established here by the 7th century, followed around 500 years later by a substantial Norman parish kirk, among Scotland's first. The handsome building we see today is, however, a largely 16th- and 17th-century structure, with extensive late Victorian restoration; little is left to conjure truly ancient times apart from a chevroned doorway in the south wall, now blocked, and a handful of tantalising, fragmentary monuments, on display in the little museum.

The most elegant are the incomplete sections of two impressively tall 8th-century crosses, carved with an orderly riot of interlacing enlivened by birds, beasts and vines, which survived only because they were reused as capstones for the parapet of a bridge over the Midhope Burn. Equally rare and intriguing are the massive 12th-century grave markers in 'hogback' style, thought to represent the roofs of longhouses or feasting halls for the dead. These mute stones may be dim shadows of their original selves, but they still speak volumes.

Address Abercorn Road, Hopetoun Estate, near South Queensferry, EH30 9SL | **Getting there** Off A 904, west of Newton; also accessible via the John Muir Way walking route and National Cycle Route 76. The museum is at the entrance to the churchyard | **Hours** Museum: accessible 24 hours (door bolted but not locked); church: Sun 10am for services | **Tip** Abercorn churchyard has some fine examples of 17th- and 18th-century gravestones carved with symbols of the trades of the deceased. Two miles away from this tranquil spot, the long-established New Hopetoun Garden Centre offers refreshment at its popular Orangery Tearoom, which has a terrace with views over themed gardens to the Firth of Forth.

63 The Bennie Museum

A communal remembrance of things past

Bathgate's memory-packed heritage centre, the Bennie Museum, owes its existence to the dedicated efforts of the community. It began in the 1970s with a campaign to save a pair of 18th-century cottages from demolition, which soon snowballed into an ambitious project, led by retired art teacher Bill Millan, to convert them into a museum of local history. With time, labour and a burgeoning collection all donated by the people of Bathgate, the remarkable result, named after the family of carters who once lived there, finally opened its doors in 1989. Still run by volunteers, the museum has since expanded into the former stables, which house a variety of vintage children's toys that must astound the TikTok generation.

While due attention is given to illustrious local figures like James Young Simpson, pioneer of anaesthetics, and James 'Paraffin' Young, father of the oil industry, most of the displays evoke ordinary folk and the often harsh reality of their daily lives, with objects ranging from a weaver's loom to a 'cutty stool' from Bathgate High Church – a low wooden seat where parishioners were shamed in front of the congregation for the sin of fornication, or for simply falling asleep during the sermon, and errant children were publicly birched.

But the most instantly eye-catching exhibit is a fine painted banner that used to be held aloft at the biggest event in Bathgate's calendar, the gala day procession, which was formerly named in honour of John Newland, an 18th-century plantation owner who left a substantial bequest to fund the construction of new schools in his native town. On the back is an image of local laird Alexander Marjoribanks, who intervened in Bathgate's favour after the will was contested by relatives. The long-running annual pageant has, however, now severed its connection with Newland, whose fortune was achieved by slave labour.

HE FOUGHT A GOOD FIGHT FOR BATHGATES RIGHTS

ALEX. MARJORIBANKS OF BALBARDIE.

Address 9–11 Mansefield Street, Bathgate, EH48 4HU, +44 (0)1506 634944, www.benniemuseum.org.uk | Getting there Train to Bathgate; bus 29, 31 73, X17, X27 or X28 to town centre | Hours Mon–Sat, Apr–Sept 11am–4pm, Oct–Mar 11am–3.30pm | Tip The Bathgate History Trail takes you round 15 town centre locations, all with informative plaques giving insights into their past significance. Two locations near the museum are the Regal Theatre, an Art Deco former cinema whose opening in 1938 was delayed due to controversy over a flamboyant plasterwork panel depicting a naked charioteer, and Bargaly House, which (in case you're hungry) now houses the popular Café Bar 1912.

64__Dreadnought Rock

Old rockers never die…

A fixture of the West Lothian music scene since the early 1970s, Dreadnought Rock is still drawing droves of enthusiastic fans from all across the Central Belt after over half a century. The much-loved Bathgate venue took its gutsy name from the town's Dreadnought Hotel, where it had its beginnings with the regular weekend takeover of one of its function rooms for a rock disco. This establishment, incidentally, had in its turn been christened in homage to a famous hotel in Callander, which has the motto of the fearsome Clan Macnab, 'Dread nought', emblazoned above its door.

Bathgate had a hugely vibrant nightlife scene in those far-off days that continued into the 1980s and '90s, and Dreadnought Rock was a key part of it, with a winning formula for a great night out that evolved with the decades, embracing new music, new audiences and new technology. In 2006, however, the old hotel closed down and the club was forced to find a new home, settling after a period of uncertainty on a building in King Street. Under the same long-serving team that had built the original Dreadnought into a phenomenon, this was customised into an ideal venue for all rock lovers, with a laid-back lower level for those who want to enjoy a drink with friends, and an upper floor for live band performances, where you can join in the excitement and dance the night away with the energetic crowd.

Whatever your preference, you'll find the environment safe, clean and relaxed – despite the preconceptions that some people have, this isn't a place that attracts hordes of head-banging leather-clad hairy bikers. In fact, its wide appeal crosses the generations, with loyal fans from the old days now bringing along their sons and daughters. The music on offer is equally broad-based, encompassing genres from punk to ska and hip-hop to heavy metal as well as the classic rock that will never die.

Address 14–16 King Street, Bathgate, EH48 1AX, +44 (0)1506 632879, www.dreadnoughtrock.com | Getting there Train to Bathgate; bus 29, 73, X18 X27 or X28 | Hours Fri & Sat 7pm–3am (last entry 1am) | Tip Bathgate's Regal Theatre is home to the Reconnect Rock School, which offers one-to-one and build-a-band lessons to youngsters on Saturdays from 10am to noon. It also runs a children's stage school, with classes in both drama and theatrical production.

65 Cairnpapple Hill
A panoramic view of prehistory

The basalt outcrop of Cairnpapple nestles quietly amid the rolling green Bathgate Hills, its broad, gently convex summit standing at a height of just over 1,000 feet. It's quite easy to access, and the short walk up from the road shouldn't leave you breathless – but the views once you get there certainly will. On a clear day you can see right across central Scotland from the Firth of Forth to the Firth of Clyde, south to the Border hills and north to the Trossachs and beyond. A mere trickle of visitors come here today, but in distant antiquity this dramatic spot was an essential destination for countless generations of local farming folk.

Cairnpapple is in fact the most significant archaeological site in mainland Scotland. Thanks to an excavation in 1947 by the legendary Stuart Piggott that was ground-breaking both literally and figuratively, this evocative setting is known to have been a focal point for rituals, ceremonial gatherings and high-class burials for an incredible four millennia.

The most impressive phase began around 3,000 B.C., with the construction of a vast henge monument, and it remained a sacred site, through many changes in belief, well into the early Christian era. Modern-day pagans still celebrate its spiritual power, and a story has lately gained currency of an elemental 'Silverman' who makes his fleet-footed way around the slopes.

The layout of the site today shows five distinct eras of prehistoric activity, which can be a bit bewildering for the non-specialist. Moreover, two dominant features date from the humdrum mid-20th century – a large concrete dome, built to protect two Bronze-Age burials and allow access for visitors, and a wartime Nissen hut, now used as an interpretation centre. But there's still an indefinable quality about the place that is remarkably compelling – the longer you stay, the more you feel its atavistic allure.

Address Bathgate Hills, EH49 7AL, +44 (0)1506 634622, www.historicenvironment.scot | **Getting there** Off minor road 1.25 miles east of Torphichen at OS map reference NS 987 717; parking in layby. The site is 0.3 mile from the road, up a flight of steps and along a grassy path | **Hours** Apr–Sept daily 10am–5pm | **Tip** Half a mile south, near the prominent crag known as the Knock, is a modern stone circle, consisting of two concentric rings of megaliths with a dolmen structure in the middle, plus a small wickerwork temple dedicated to Persephone. The charming complex was built in 1998, as a 50th birthday gift, by the son of the farmer who owned the site.

66_ The Korean War Memorial

Remembering the fallen of the Forgotten War

The war that erupted in 1950 in the divided country of Korea raged for three years and led to over a million combat casualties. It began when the South was invaded by the Soviet-occupied North; the United Nations reacted by sending forces from 20 countries to aid its defence, while China supported the North. The fierce and brutal fighting concluded in uneasy stalemate, and the country remains partitioned into two hostile states.

Though many will remember that this was the nominal backdrop for the TV sitcom *M*A*S*H*, the real-life conflict is sadly absent from public consciousness. Few are aware that around 90,000 UK service personnel were deployed (a number second only to those of the USA) or that it cost the lives of over a thousand Britons – many of them teenagers doing their obligatory National Service. The veterans who returned in 1953 met with widespread indifference in a worn-out nation struggling to emerge from the long shadow of World War II, and it would be decades before the sacrifice of the fallen was recognised with a memorial.

The most striking of the few national monuments to the war that now exist is the shrine in the Bathgate Hills, created by the Lothians and West of Scotland branch of the British Korean Veterans Association and dedicated in June 2000. In a peaceful enclave amid rolling green uplands, reminiscent of the steep terrain where the war was fought, is an arboretum of 1,100 native Scottish trees, one for every British serviceman killed. At its heart are twin mounds in the form of the yin-yang symbol, planted with 110 Korean firs grown from seed in Scotland. Between them is an evocative memorial pavilion, roofed with traditional Korean tiles, where all the Britons killed are named, including merchant seamen and war correspondents. It's a uniquely poignant endeavour to redress our shameful amnesia about this Forgotten War.

Address Witchcraig Wood, near Torphichen, EH48 4NW | **Getting there** On a minor road off the B 792, 1.6 miles east of Torphichen; signposted from Linlithgow and Bathgate, and from the M 8 and M 9 | **Hours** Accessible 24 hours | **Tip** Continue your walk uphill through Witchcraig Wood to the spectacular viewpoint at Witchcraig Wall, a small enclosure and resting place made up of 43 different types of local rock that illustrate the geological diversity of the region. Nearby is the medieval Refuge Stone, which marks the limit of the sanctuary belonging to Torphichen Preceptory.

67 Dalmeny Kirk

Fantastic beasts and where to find them

Just eight miles from Edinburgh city centre, and flanked by busy transport links, Dalmeny has sprawled in recent years as a modern commuter suburb. At its core, however, is an old village with a tranquil, rural feel, all the more surprising for a place that was once a centre of the shale oil industry. There are neat rows of traditional 19th-century cottages, built for workers on the Dalmeny estate, and a village green – an uncommon boon in Scotland. But dominating the scene is a very much rarer sight – a 12th-century parish church in richly ornamented Romanesque style, which has survived with few alterations and is still in use today. The tower alone is recent, added in 1937 to replace an original that had collapsed 500 years earlier.

Dedicated to St Cuthbert, the kirk was commissioned by Gospatric III, Earl of Lothian. Its grandeur seems due to its site near the Forth crossing at Queensferry, which must have made it a regular stop for pilgrims *en route* to St Andrews. The interior is a serene, elegant space, its arches and vaulting embellished with splendid zigzag mouldings supported by grotesque carved heads. But it's the exterior, at the south entrance, where the stone masons really went to town, adorning the archway with exquisite figurative imagery, now much weathered but still powerfully compelling. The inner panels depict a series of mythical creatures including the phoenix, basilisk, dragon and griffin, all based on illustrations from a bestiary, a kind of encyclopaedia of animals, real and imaginary, which endowed the supposed attributes of each beast with Christian meaning and used tales about them to teach moral lessons. The symbolism of these carvings, which would have been painted, emphasised the mystical significance of the doorway to folk of medieval times: this was a portal where they left the ordinary world and entered the realm of the divine.

Address Main Street, Dalmeny, EH30 9TT, +44 (0)131 331 1100, www.dalmeny.org |
Getting there Train to Dalmeny and a 15-minute walk; bus 43 to Dalmeny Village
Hall | Hours Exterior: always accessible; interior: open for services Sun 11am | Tip The
picturesque churchyard is well worth exploring. There are several fine 17th- and 18th-
century gravestones decorated with *Memento Mori* motifs such as the skull and crossed
bones (which have nothing to do with pirates!), and opposite the south door is a massive
carved stone coffin, thought to have once held the remains of the church's builder.

68 King Tom

Noble memorial to the Monarch of Mentmore

Equestrian statues – ponderous bronzes of long-dead generals or monarchs mounted on subordinate chargers – are two a penny, strutting their stuff in so many city squares. But life-sized monuments that honour horses *per se*, unburdened by riders, are much rarer beasts, mostly found only at racecourses. So it's a delightful surprise to come upon a fine specimen standing in solitary splendour on the peaceful green acres of the Dalmeny estate.

The equine hero in question is King Tom (1851–78), a racehorse famed as the 'foundation stallion' of the stud farm created by Baron Mayer de Rothschild on his 3,000-acre estate of Mentmore in Buckinghamshire. A scion of the vastly wealthy banking dynasty, 'Muffy' (as he was familiarly known) was a lover of 'the turf', a member of the exclusive Jockey Club and a keen horseman himself, despite weighing 16 stone. He bought King Tom as a juvenile for the considerable sum of £2,000, and after being retired from racing at the age of four, the stallion, nicknamed the Monarch of Mentmore, went on to prove his worth, siring a string of winning progeny during his brilliant career 'standing at stud'. At 16 hands, Tom was a big horse, but he was noted for his amenable disposition – a fan who met him at the 'lusty old age' of 20 was impressed by the 'most gracious manner' of the 'good-tempered giant'.

On Tom's death in 1878, the Baron commissioned a likeness in bronze from one of the most respected portrait sculptors of the day, Joseph Boehm, whose many illustrious human sitters included Queen Victoria. For over a century the memorial stood on the grassy mound at Mentmore where Tom is buried, but in 1982, after the sale of the estate, it was transferred to Dalmeny, home of the descendants of the Baron's daughter Hannah. He's a long way from his stables now, and a bit the worse for wear, but it's a lovely place to be put out to grass.

Address Dalmeny Estate, near South Queensferry, EH30 TQ, +44 (0)131 331 1888, www.roseberyestates.co.uk | Getting there Bus 43 to Easter Dalmeny and a 20-minute walk from estate entrance; the statue is on a rise just east of Dalmeny House | Hours Accessible 24 hours | Tip Dalmeny Estate boasts a spectacular 4.5 mile walking route along the shore of the Firth of Forth. It starts at the Hawes Inn, South Queensferry and runs to Cramond, on the north-west edge of Edinburgh, passing close to King Tom on the way. The ornate Tudor-Gothic Dalmeny House contains objects from Mentmore among its fine collections of art and antiques.

69 Bangour Hospital Village
Care in a community

In 1898, an unusual development began to take shape on the country estate of Bangour. The rolling green acres had just been purchased by the Edinburgh District Lunacy Board; despite their antiquated name, they had an enlightened vision of patient care, and their project was a radical new facility for the treatment of the mentally ill. The healthy rural setting was part of its ethos, which was modelled on the 'colony' system developed in Germany in the 1870s. Rather than a grim prison-like institution, the hospital would operate as a self-contained, self-sufficient community, with patients housed in attractive domestic-style residences, and employed in therapeutic farm work and useful trades. The completed 'village' was widely praised by the medical establishment, but it also had powerful critics: at the official opening in 1906, former prime minister Lord Rosebery blustered furiously about the cost of providing 'sumptuous homes' for the 'intellectually dead'.

The architect was the eminent Hippolyte Blanc, whose Scots-Renaissance design included 32 individual villas, each designed for 25 to 40 patients, a recreation hall, a shop in rural cottage style, a sports pavilion and even a railway station, as well as medical blocks and a nurses' home. Completing the picture is an unexpectedly grand church, although this dates from the 1920s, and was built in recognition of the vital role the hospital played in World War I, when it was requisitioned for wounded soldiers.

Bangour Hospital remained in operation for almost a century before it was finally closed in 2004, and the deserted village soon fell into disrepair. There was concern about its future, until in 2023 work began on a housing development incorporating the most important historic buildings – Bangour Village Estate, an 'aspirational new neighbourhood' offering a 'unique environmentally friendly way of life'.

Address Bangour, Dechmont, EH52 6LL | Getting there Off A 89, 2.5 miles south-west of Uphall | Tip Five miles east is the lovely Almondell and Calderwood Country Park, covering 220 acres formerly owned by two separate families of the landed gentry. Established in 1969, it was the first facility of its kind in West Lothian, and features delightful woodland and riverside walks with abundant flora and fauna, as well as a Visitor Centre.

70 King Jamie's Silver Mines

A brief bonanza that brought right royal ridicule

One fine June day in 1606, a Linlithgowshire miner was prospecting for coal at Hilderston when he made a much more momentous discovery – silver, running through the red ore in bright filaments 'like unto the haire of a man's head'. Local landowner Sir Thomas Hamilton quickly obtained a lease to extract the mineral; it proved to be a rich vein of exceptional purity, and before long the first shaft, christened 'God's Blessing', was being worked by 59 men.

Scots had a special penchant for the precious metal, though hitherto they'd relied on foreign sources of supply – and recycling. This tradition originated over a thousand years earlier, when native craftsmen began reworking Roman 'hacksilver' hoarded by tribal chiefs into high status jewellery. The thrifty custom of turning old silver into fashionable new items continued for centuries.

The Hilderston find soon excited the curiosity of King James VI, then three years into his simultaneous tenure of the throne of England. James took a personal interest in mining technology, which in the popular mind was driven chiefly by his extravagance and love of prestigious jewellery. At first, he received a tenth of the profits from Hilderston, but in 1608, after reports of its 'inexhaustible' supply of rich ore, he commandeered the site for the Crown and expanded operations. It soon became clear, however, that the bonanza was over and little silver remained. News of the affair travelled widely, even reaching the ears of the Doge of Venice. In London it inspired a satirical play, lampooning James' practice of lavishing wealth on his male 'favourites', which the furious king closed down.

All that's left of the royal venture are a few hollows in a field, but there are more substantial remains of historic limestone workings, which help to evoke an image of the feverish industry that once engulfed this tranquil site.

Address Near Hilderston, Bathgate Hills, EH48 4NW | Getting there Follow directions for Cairnpapple; the old mine workings are about 100 yards further down the road, along the valley of the burn at the foot of the hill | Hours Always accessible | Tip A mile and a half south, at Limefield on the edge of Bathgate, is the old quarry of East Kirkton, another site famous for a remarkable geological find. It was here in 1984 that amateur fossil hunter Stan Wood discovered the 340-million-year-old *Westlothiana Lizziae*, aka Lizzie the lizard, a specimen (now in the National Museum of Scotland) that sparked a total rethink of reptilian evolution.

71 Military Museum Scotland

Lest we forget

When ex-soldier Ian Inglis first sought support to turn his huge collection of military memorabilia into a visitor attraction, he faced a barrage of disdain. People told him he lacked the necessary education and experience, and that it wouldn't last six months. Undaunted, he persevered with his passion project, opening the doors of his new museum in 2017, and triumphing over his detractors as it went on to win six awards in as many years. Unlike other military museums it's not affiliated to any regiment, which is in fact one of its strengths.

Ian's interest in all things military was sparked at the tender age of nine, when his father died and he inherited the medals from his wartime service with the Royal Artillery. He later joined the army himself, serving for 21 years while continuing to collect artefacts relating to Scotland's military heritage from World War I to the present day. By the 2010s he had amassed an astonishing 100,000 items, including uniforms, kit, photographs and letters as well as weapons ranging from bayonets to Bren guns. After a request to show some material to local kids, he began taking a travelling collection around schools in West Lothian, and the success of these visits inspired him to find a site to put it on permanent display.

There really is something for everyone among the chock-a-block exhibits, from an eye-catching Remembrance Day dress made from thousands of crocheted poppies to a superb scale model depicting a key action during the Battle of Passchendaele. Vivid outdoor displays include recreations of a trench from the Western Front and a field kitchen, as well as army vehicles. You'll find information on war poets (male and female), and on the role of animals in wartime, including the mascot bear Winnipeg who gave his name to Winnie-the-Pooh. The lovingly curated museum is greatly enhanced by the input of veterans who are regularly on hand to chat, since it also functions as a drop-in hub for ex-service personnel.

Within the image: MIND YOUR HEAD · TO THE FRONT · Poets Corner · MINES

Address Legion Hall, Louis Braille Avenue, Wilkieston, EH27 8DU, +44 (0)7799 565243, www.facebook.com/milmussco | **Getting there** Bus X 22, X 27 or X 40 to Wilkieston Post Office | **Hours** Tue, Wed & Fri – Sun, 10am – 4pm (Mon & Thu school & group bookings only) | **Tip** The Cyrenians Farm at nearby Kirknewton is a social enterprise venture run by a long-established homelessness charity. With a belief in the power of food to change lives for the better, and an orchard with over 25 varieties of heritage apples, it supplies organic, home-grown fruit, vegetables and other produce via a local delivery scheme, and organises workshops on a range of green skills.

72 Beecraigs Country Park
Unwind in the uplands

When it comes to exhilarating green spaces, Linlithgow is sitting pretty. Just a couple of miles south of the historic town centre and its magical lochside sward lie the rolling Bathgate Hills, home to West Lothian's largest country park, Beecraigs. Much valued by locals, but far enough from major roads to be off the radar of visitors passing through, the 370-hectare upland expanse has such an atmosphere of secluded tranquillity that it's easy to forget how close it is to the conurbations of both Falkirk and Edinburgh.

Well-made trails for walkers and cyclists lead through swathes of coniferous woodland, meadows and farmland and round an attractive fishing loch, with far-reaching vistas and glimpses of wildlife near at hand adding to the sense of remoteness from urban life. Added attractions include a field archery centre, an adventure playground and barbecues for hire. There's also a camping site near the Visitor Centre, which has a café and gift shop.

It's surprising to learn how recently Beecraigs took on the appearance it has today. The loch is in fact artificial, built between 1914 and 1918 by German prisoners of war to serve as a reservoir for the local water supply. At that time the country was largely unwooded farmland with a mix of rough grazing and arable fields, and it was only in 1922 that the first pine and spruce trees were planted to act as a shelterbelt. More extensive conifer plantations were added over the next 50 years, and in 1977 the remaining farm acquired a deer herd, which grew to become one of the attractions after Beecraigs officially opened as a country park in 1980.

On the western edge is Cockleroy, an easily climbed hill of 912 feet with the remains of an Iron Age hillfort at the top, and fabulous views in every direction. The quaint name is said by some to derive from its resemblance to a hat worn by James V when he was presented with a French order of chivalry, the Golden Cockle.

Address Near Linlithgow, EH49 6PL, +44 (0)1506 284516, www.westlothian.gov.uk/article/34121/beecraigs-country-park | **Getting there** Train to Linlithgow; bus 31, F 45, F 49 or X 38 to town centre. There's a walking route to the park from the Union Canal basin that leads up Manse Road, along Dark Entry (a road closed to traffic) and then up Preston Road via a bridle path (2.7 miles) | **Hours** Unrestricted; Visitor Centre: summer 9am–7pm, winter 10am–4pm | **Tip** For many years there was a working farm at Beecraigs with rare breeds of livestock. This has sadly gone, but anyone keen on Highland Cattle (and who isn't?) can see them at Muiravonside Country Park near Whitecross. Their fold – the correct collective name for this irresistible breed – includes several that were formerly kept at Beecraigs.

73 __ The Crown Spire
The fearsome geometry that became a local icon

St Michael's, Linlithgow, is one of the largest and finest medieval churches in Scotland. Spectacularly located on a hillock overlooking the loch, right next to the palace, it was begun in 1425 on the site of an earlier kirk destroyed by fire. In a culminating flourish of civic pride, its west tower was topped with a massive openwork steeple in the shape of a royal crown. But by 1820, after centuries of battering by the elements, the intricate stonework was in imminent danger of collapse, and the spire was taken down. A programme of restoration in the 1890s did not include its restitution, and the parish kirk continued to languish without its crowning glory for over 140 years.

It was in the early 1960s, during the dynamic ministry of the Rev Dr David Steel (father of the politician of the same name), that a replacement spire was at last proposed. There was insufficient cash to fund its construction in stone, but Steel seized this setback as an opportunity for the church to make a bold statement, in modern materials and a radical style relevant to the new era. The commission was given to Geoffrey Clarke, a major figure among the generation of post-war sculptors whose spiky, angst-ridden creations had gained the tag 'the geometry of fear'. Clarke's credentials included extensive work at Coventry Cathedral, and this fed into his design for the Linlithgow spire – a symbolic, 56-foot representation of Christ's crown of thorns, in laminated wood clad in golden-hued aluminium.

Like all modernist projects it attracted controversy, made worse by its visibility from the Glasgow to Edinburgh railway line. It was likened to a missile set for launch, or a huge wigwam – and Clarke himself was never happy with the final colour, which he thought 'brassy'. But six decades on, no one can imagine the town without its thorny emblem, now triumphantly gleaming again after a major refurbishment scheme, completed in 2024.

Address St Michael's Church, Kirkgate, Linlithgow, EH49 7AL | Getting there Train to Linlithgow; bus 31, F45 or X38 to Linlithgow Cross | Hours Always visible; church open Sat & Sun 11am–1pm | Tip The flamboyantly decorative Cross Well fountain dominates the square at the foot of Kirkgate. Carved in 1807 by one-handed mason Robert Gray (who worked with a mallet strapped to his left stump), it's a faithful replica of a 17th-century original, incorporating charming figurative carvings into a crown design that echoes the long-gone original spire of St Michael's Church.

74_House of the Binns
The dynamic Dalyell dynasty

Don't be put off by the unfortunate-sounding name. Binns is just an old Scots word for hills, describing the estate's upland setting, and this is in fact as agreeable a country mansion as you could ever wish to visit. It's still home to the Dalyell family after more than 400 years, though it's been in the care of the National Trust for Scotland since 1944. Their passionately knowledgeable guides bring the late inhabitants to vivid life as they take you round the invitingly liveable rooms and their richly storied contents.

The house was begun in 1612 by Thomas Dalyell, an aspirational butter merchant who found favour with James VI and became his Master of the Rolls (no, not that kind). Despite later remodelling – the 'toy fort' façade was added in 1812 – it remains substantially his creation. Several rooms boast 17th-century wooden panelling and chimney pieces, and there's even a secret passage. Most impressive are the chambers upstairs, adorned in 1630 with exuberant plasterwork ceilings in the vain hope of a visit by Charles I.

But it is the next laird, General Tam, who dominates the narrative. A Royalist who vowed never to shave again after the fall of the Stuarts, he escaped to Russia and distinguished himself in service to the Tsar, though once back home he became infamous for his cruel treatment of the dissenting Covenanters. It's said he played cards with the Devil – and won – at a marble table that still bears a furious hoofmark, and his swanky cavalry boots allegedly have a life of their own. You'll also hear tales of more engaging Dalyells like Sir John, a naturalist who kept a sea anemone as a pet, and the 20th-century Tam, a highly principled Labour politician.

Peacocks roam the surrounding parkland, and there are lovely walks with panoramic vistas across the Forth to Fife and beyond, and south to the Pentland Hills. The prominent tower is a folly, built by 5th baronet James as the result of an after-dinner wager.

Address Binns View, near Linlithgow, EH49 7NA, +44 (0)1506 830175, www.nts.org/visit/places/house-of-binns | Getting there Off A 904, three miles east of Linlithgow | Hours House: Apr–Sept, guided tours only, see website for days and times (booking essential); estate: daily 9am–7.30pm | Tip On the A 904, just a mile from The Binns, Mannerston's is a pleasantly airy family-run café and deli, with artisan ice cream in a range of intriguing flavours as well as more substantial, healthy fare.

75 Linlithgow Canal Centre

A leisurely outing on the Mathematical River

Of all Linlithgow's attractions, the most surprising is surely the delightful waterway that runs unobtrusively through the town, high above its historic centre. It's a location that seems counterintuitive, but then the Union Canal is no ordinary waterway. Commissioned in 1818 to link Edinburgh with the Forth–Clyde Canal at Falkirk, and create a through route to Glasgow, it follows the 240-foot contour line for its whole 32-mile length, thus dispensing with the need for locks, speeding the flow of traffic, and earning it the nickname 'The Mathematical River'. Though its chief purpose was to transport coal, it also transformed passenger travel: swift horse-drawn barges made it possible to do the Edinburgh–Glasgow journey in just seven hours, and in comfort unknown to road users. A charming guide published in 1823 describes the impressive sights to be seen along the way, as well as the intriguing prospect of 'observing the motley group of persons' on board.

But the Union Canal's heyday was short-lived: just 20 years after its completion, an intercity railway was opened, which took away most of its traffic; a long decline followed, culminating in its closure to navigation in 1965. A few years later, however, Linlithgow councillor Mel Gray started a campaign to restore the local section for leisure use, which led to the formation in 1975 of the town's Union Canal Society. They began acquiring and restoring vessels for conversion to passenger boats, and put together a fascinating little museum.

Still thriving half a century on, the group operates regular short trips on its 12-seater flagship *Victoria*, plus excursions on larger boats to the soaring Avon Aqueduct and even as far as the Falkirk Wheel, the vast boat lift whose inauguration in 2002 re-established the east-west canal link. At a steady three miles per hour, it's a blissfully relaxing way to travel.

Address Manse Road Basin, Linlithgow, EH49 6AJ, www.lucs.org.uk | **Getting there** Train to Linlithgow and a five-minute walk uphill from the station | **Hours** Short boat trips, museum & café: Apr–Sept Sat & Sun, also Mon–Fri in July & early Aug, 1.30–4.30pm. See website for details of longer cruises (Sat & Sun only, booking advisable) | **Tip** On the opposite bank of the canal basin, look out for the statue of Dudley the cat, erected in 2018 in memory of his owner, Liz Burrows, a generous supporter of the town's Burgh Beautiful project.

76__Linlithgow Loch

Man-made islands, dancing birds and a faithful dog

The glorious expanse of fresh water that skirts the ancient burgh of Linlithgow is fundamental to the town's existence, as is reflected in the 'lin' part of its name, which means 'loch'. It's an extraordinary asset to find so close to an urban centre – just a couple of minutes' walk from the busy High Street, but screened from view by buildings and trees, which adds a frisson of surprise to the joy of a relaxing stroll by its shores. There's also an undeniable sensation of privilege, for the land that contains it, known as the Peel, was once a royal park, serving the Renaissance pleasure palace that dominates the skyline.

The largest natural loch in the whole of the Lothians, it's what geologists call a kettle hole, a shallow basin carved out over 10,000 years ago by a block of ice from a retreating glacier. Intriguingly, the two islets that punctuate its surface are not natural, but the remains of artificial crannogs, large timber round-houses on wooden stilts, constructed around 500 B.C.

In later history, its waters became a crucial resource for local people, not only for the food they provided but as a driver of early industries such as leather tanning and linen manufacture. Today it's valued as a facility for boating and water sports and, above all, as a haven for wildlife. A variety of visiting birds can be spotted at different seasons, and there are breeding populations of the elegant great crested grebe (whose courtship dance is a sight to behold) and the graceful mute swan.

The much-loved loch also features in a Linlithgow legend that derives from an image on the town's medieval burgh seal. It tells of a black female hound that swam its waters to deliver food to her owner, who was imprisoned on one of the islands. In honour of her heroism, townsfolk of whatever gender proudly maintain the custom of referring to themselves as Black Bitches.

Address Water Yett Car Park, Linlithgow, EH49 7HN, is a good place to begin a circuit of the loch (2.25 miles) – an easy walk on level paths | **Getting there** Train to Linlithgow; bus 31, F45, F49 or X38 to Linlithgow High Street | **Tip** The independent, volunteer-run Linlithgow Museum is a must if you want to explore the past of this fascinating old burgh – and indeed its future. The most unusual exhibit must certainly be the blue plaque commemorating fictional native son Montgomery Scott, better known as *Star Trek*'s Scotty, who will apparently be born in the town on 28 June in the year 2222.

77 Linlithgow Palace
Idyllic retreat for Renaissance royalty

Scotland has no shortage of romantic ruins with royal connections, but even within this context Linlithgow Palace is in a class of its own. Set like a jewel on its exquisite lochside site, it was once among the finest residences in Europe – splendid enough to enchant Mary of Guise, second wife of James V, who was used to the sumptuous châteaux of her native France. It was here that she gave birth to Scotland's most famous monarch, Mary, Queen of Scots. Though long since a roofless shell, shorn of its ornamentation, statuary and stained glass, it remains a majestic expression of the power and sophistication of the Stewart kings.

A royal manor had existed on the site since the 12th century, but it was James I who seized the opportunity of transforming it into a pleasure palace in the continental fashion after it was damaged by fire in 1424. The chief glory of this period was the Great Hall, a vast function room for entertaining guests in magnificent style, well equipped for the local climate with a huge three-bay fireplace. The next significant phase of building was under the cultured James IV, who completed the royal apartments in time for the lavish celebrations to mark his marriage to Margaret Tudor in 1503. Inspired by this festival, re-enactment events now take place every July on the Peel (the grassy sward below the palace) with spectacular and highly entertaining jousting, falconry and living history demonstrations.

But the palace's most impressive permanent feature is one of the improvements added by his son, James V – the fountain in the central courtyard, which he commissioned in 1537, perhaps as a gift for his new French queen. A *tour de force* of both hydraulic engineering and sculpture, the elaborate three-tiered structure is adorned with a glorious gallimaufry of mythical beasts and curious human figures, symbolically topped with a crown.

Address Kirkgate, Linlithgow, EH49 7AL, +44 (0)1506 842896, www.historicenvironment.scot/visit-a-place/places/linlithgow-palace | Getting there Train to Linlithgow; bus 31, F 45, F 49 or X 38 to Linlithgow Cross | Hours Daily, Apr – Sept 9.30am – 5pm, Oct – Mar 10am – 4pm | Tip Il Fruttivendolo is an Italian greengrocer and delicatessen at 211 High Street that has been bringing a taste of European quality to Linlithgow since 2020. It stocks an exceptional range of seasonal fruit and veg, much of it sourced from owner Francesco Cosentino's native Sicily, plus pastries, cheeses, cured meats and other authentic Italian specialities that you won't find elsewhere in the area.

78 Almond Valley

Eclectic heritage and fun for all ages

Much more than a regular heritage centre, Almond Valley is a remarkable blend of working farm, industrial museum and adventure playground, all on a pleasant wooded site that extends for almost a mile along the Livingston riverside. It's a winning combination, with so much to see and do that a single day isn't enough.

Established in 1985, the attraction grew out of a project to preserve the steadings, paddocks and 18th-century watermill of an abandoned farm near Livingston village and restore them to working life. Then in 1990, as the phoenix of Livingston New Town continued to spread its wings over the changing landscape, the site was chosen for a purpose-built museum dedicated to shale oil, the long-gone industry that dominated West Lothian for over a century. Soon afterwards, a narrow-gauge railway was added to the mix, with cute locomotives that belie their industrial origins.

The history of shale mining might sound like a subject strictly for specialists, but this museum turns it into a voyage of discovery for all ages, beginning with aeons-old fossils and the rocks that were exploited to make West Lothian the site (in 1850) of the world's first oil works, and ending with the broader social history of how the industry impacted the local area.

The farm is arranged to allow visitors a close-up view of an endearing variety of sheep, goats, cattle, horses and poultry, many of them rare breeds, plus some gorgeous alpacas and a surprise giant tortoise. As well as talks and demonstrations from the friendly staff, there's a programme of seasonal activities for all ages, and a huge range of imaginatively themed play facilities where kids can enjoy doing their own thing. The latest addition is the Ruined Peel, a three-storeyed adventure inspired by the medieval castle that once stood nearby. If only all heritage centres were as much fun as Almond Valley!

Address Millfield, Livingston, EH54 7AR, +44 (0)1506 414957, www.almondvalley.co.uk |
Getting there Train to Livingston North and a 30-minute walk; bus 7, 26, 31, X 24, X 25,
X 27 or X 28 to town centre and a long but refreshing walk along riverside paths | Hours
Daily 10am – 5pm | Tip The original Livingston village is a charming conservation area,
with many 18th-century buildings and an atmospheric churchyard that's much older. At its
heart is the historic Livingston Inn, an award-winning pub with accommodation. Robert
Burns once stayed here, and apparently dallied with a local lassie, to whom he dedicated a
salacious song, *The Lass o' Liviston*.

79 The Dechmont UFO Trail

If you go down to the woods today…

Few goings-on in Livingston have ever made international headlines, but the ordeal experienced by forester Bob Taylor on 9 November 1979 was so extraordinary that it has fascinated the world's media ever since. Bob was going about his work in woodland at Dechmont when, he claimed, he was attacked by an alien spaceship, a 'flying dome' that sent out two spiked metal spheres which grabbed his legs. He then passed out. When he returned home later in a bewildered and dishevelled state, his wife phoned the local constabulary, who treated the incident as a criminal assault.

There are several factors that mark this as a rare event in the annals of ufology. It took place in broad daylight, on a bright morning, it did not begin with a strange light in the sky – and it's the only such occurrence in the world that has been subject to a police investigation. The case was never solved, though forensic scientists concluded that rips in Bob's trousers were the result of mechanical action, hooking on to the fabric and dragging it upwards.

In 1979, the success of the film *Close Encounters of the Third Kind* had no doubt fired the public appetite for tales of extraterrestrials. But Bob was a quiet, publicity-shy man, and no one – colleagues, police, reporters or UFO sceptics – ever doubted that he was honestly relating what he thought had happened. Throughout his life (he died, aged 88, in 2007) he never deviated from any detail of his account. The incident continues to defy rational explanation, despite numerous attempts to debunk his story, some of them almost as far-fetched as the alien landing hypothesis.

The clearing where it all took place is half the size now, and the trees have grown considerably. The rustle and creak of the swaying boughs and shifting, dappled light lend an air of uneasy mystery to the site, which is marked by a memorial boulder and an information board that will leave you even more baffled.

Address Dechmont Woods, Deans, Livingston, EH54 8PS | **Getting there** Train to Livingston North; bus X25, X28 or 280 to Deans Community High School; a waymarked trail leads uphill from the car park at the end of Eastwood Park, past Dechmont Law to the site (c. 20 minutes) | **Hours** Accessible 24 hours | **Tip** It's just 15 miles (as the saucer flies) from Dechmont to Scotland's main hotspot for UFO sightings – the small town of Bonnybridge, cornerstone of the zone known to paranormal enthusiasts as the Falkirk Triangle. Since 1992 there have been many hundreds of reports from this area of unexplained lights in the sky and mysterious flying objects.

80 Livingston Skate Park

Ride the concrete wave at legendary Livi

In 1981, a little piece of Southern California took root in the heart of West Lothian, with the opening of a state-of-the-art skate park in Livingston New Town. The UK's skateboarding craze was by then past its peak, and many commercial parks had already closed down. But Livi (as it was soon nicknamed) was different. It was the culmination of a campaign for a purpose-built facility begun five years earlier by local skater Kenny Omond, and brought to fruition by maverick architect Iain Urquhart. His considered approach was to actively involve skaters themselves at every stage of the project, incorporating both their ideas and their ethos into his concept for a free, unsupervised outdoor amenity, open 24 hours.

Though it's now an Olympic sport, skateboarding's appeal remains that of an unstructured, non-competitive youth subculture. It originated in 1950s California as an offshoot of surfing, but its development from a casual sidewalk activity into a major recreation began during a serious drought that afflicted the state in 1975, leaving swimming pools unfilled. The most fashionable of these, in the kidney shape made famous by Finnish architect Alvar Aalto, had organically curved basins that made them ideal for creative (and illicit) skating. This serendipity had a massive influence on the development of the sport.

Iain Urquhart's thorough research naturally took him to Californian parks; there he built a rapport with skating pioneers like Tony Hawk, who would later return the compliment by visiting Livingston to give his creation an active seal of approval. It soon gained iconic status at an international level, and was key to establishing the Scottish skate scene of the time as the most vibrant in Europe. Now, with the patina of over four decades, Livi is revered as a historic monument, while still attracting enthusiasts of all ages from both near and far.

Address 4 Almondside, Livingston, EH54 6QU | Getting there Bus 7, 26, 31, X24, X25, X27 or X28 to Livingston (Club Earth Nightclub) | Hours Open 24 hours | Tip Get away from the concrete and into woodland greenery with a relaxing walk on the signposted paths along the nearby River Almond – or, if you're keen on top brands and in search of a bargain, visit the famous Livingston Designer Outlet, half a mile away.

81__The Burryman

A prickly character with mysterious ancient roots

South Queensferry tends to be dominated by its panoramic outlook on the Firth of Forth and its monumental bridges. But for one day in August that magnificent trio is eclipsed, as all eyes turn to the spectacle unfolding in the town itself. Heralded by cries of 'Hip, hip hooray – it's the Burryman's Day!', a misshapen figure in a greenish-brown costume and floral bonnet lumbers through the streets, flanked by two helpers carrying flower-bedecked staffs to support his outstretched arms. He can't lower them, as he's covered from head to foot in sticky burrs – thousands of them – pressed on to his clothing that morning by family and friends, and clinging to him with a velcro-like grip.

It is to these prickly little customers – seed heads of the burdock plant (a type of thistle) – that the Burryman owes his name. Some claim it also recalls his original role, either as a 'burgh man' beating the bounds of the parish, or even as a *bourreau* – executioner and social pariah. In days gone by, similar burr-clad characters were paraded around other east coast fishing communities, including Buckie and Fraserburgh, in rituals to guarantee good fortune, or as scapegoats to purge evil. But the Queensferry Burryman is the only one to have survived into this century. And though no one can say for sure why or when the tradition originated, the local men who take on his unique mantle consider it a great honour.

These days his duties are limited to suffering the extreme discomfort of his itchy suit for a nine-hour walkabout, with mandatory stops at a series of hostelries and prominent addresses during which, although unable to eat, sit down or indeed 'answer the call of nature', he is obliged to drink up to 20 nips of whisky, through a straw. Up close, he's an uncanny, heart-pounding sight that you won't forget. Reach out and touch him gently, and he might just bring you luck.

Address South Queensferry, EH30, www.facebook.com/theburryman | Getting there
Bus 43 or 63 to South Queensferry; train to Dalmeny | Hours 2nd Fri in Aug, 9am–6pm.
It's the first event of the Ferry Fair gala week; local shops sell programmes with details of
route and timings | Tip The picturesque, two-tier High Street is a good place to catch the
Burryman during the last two hours of his walkabout. While you're waiting, grab an ice
cream from the deservedly popular Little Parlour (52 High Street). Queensferry Museum is
also well worth a visit; displays include a replica Burryman, known as Frank.

82 Hopetoun House

Gracious living for the Georgian gentry

More of a palace than a mere stately home, Hopetoun House has attracted a constant stream of superlatives since it was completed in 1767. In a guidebook published two years later, influential traveller Thomas Pennant declared it the handsomest house he'd seen in Great Britain, while other contemporary enthusiasts thought it the equal of Versailles.

Today's visitors are no less effusive in their praise, including those whose chief motivation for stopping by is to tick off the sites used as backdrops for the *Outlander* TV series. The only dismissive view on record seems to be that of the late Duke of Edinburgh who, in a typically blunt quip, described it as a 'very thin' house – though actually you can see what he meant. Hopetoun was designed above all to make a grand impact from afar, and the wings that extend on either side of the central block are very much longer than they are deep – in fact its west frontage was recently certified as having the longest garden façade of any country house in the UK.

Hopetoun has changed little since its Georgian heyday, and the Hope family still live here as they have done for over 300 years. It was completed over many decades, in a clever marriage between two distinct styles that reflect the developing aspirations of the Scottish aristocracy in the aftermath of the country's union with England. The house that forms its core was built between 1699 and 1703 by innovative architect Sir William Bruce, but less than 20 years later the multi-talented William Adam was commissioned to enlarge and remodel it in keeping with the fashion of the times, a project continued after his death by his even more gifted son Robert, who created its sublime Neoclassical interiors with his brother John.

Setting off the gracious pile to glorious effect is an expansive designed landscape that also set trends for the future.

Address Near South Queensferry, EH30 9SL, +44 (0)131 331 2451, www.hopetoun.co.uk |
Getting there Two miles west of South Queensferry along the coast road. Drivers with
Sat Nav are advised to aim for Farquhar Terrace, EH30 9RW, then continue out of the
town along Society Road, following the brown signposts. No buses stop anywhere near the
house. | Hours Apr–Sept, Thu–Mon 11am–5pm | Tip There are wonderful walks to be
had in the grounds, but if you fancy getting away from the managed pleasures of the estate,
park at nearby Society Point and explore the Hopetoun Foreshore. It's an important site of
geodiversity, with an unusually diverse array of rock formations that can be appreciated even
if you're not a specialist.

83__ The Queensferry Crossing
Setting Forth for a third time

The narrows on the Firth of Forth that became known as the Queensferry Passage must have been a crossing point from time immemorial, but it is the 11th-century Queen Margaret to whom it owes its name. She established its first regular ferryboat service, for pilgrims journeying to St Andrews. By the 1780s the crossing had become the 'most frequented' in Scotland, and demands were already being made for a bridge to ease congestion.

The passage has since morphed into a vast 'transport corridor', with no fewer than three marvels of engineering spanning the route. Since 1890 the railway has been carried by the sturdy icon that will always be *the* Forth Bridge; it wasn't until 1964, however, that the ferry was supplanted by the long-awaited Road Bridge. A state-of-the-art suspension bridge, it was intended to last for 120 years, but the volume and weight of traffic rocketed over the decades to such levels that by 2007 it was clear that the prematurely ageing structure could no longer cope. And so the decision was taken to construct a replacement further upstream, as a seamless link for the M90 motorway.

The chosen solution was an elegant three-towered, cable-stayed bridge, which gained designer Naeem Hussain a rightful induction into the Engineering Hall of Fame. Opened in 2017, it was christened the Queensferry Crossing by public vote, though local kids – personifying the existing pair as Mr and Mrs Bridges – took to calling the new arrival Kevin, after the popular Scottish comedian. Like its predecessors, the Crossing is a record-breaker: with towers over 650 feet high, it's the UK's tallest bridge, and its 1.7-mile span makes it the longest of its type in the world. But you don't have to be a technical buff to appreciate its beauty, with rows of gleaming cables fanning out like sails by day, and picked out at night like a giant trinity of skeletal manta rays.

Address Firth of Forth, EH30 9ST | **Getting there** To drive across the bridge, follow the M 90 north from Edinburgh. For a good viewpoint on the shore, take bus 43 or 63 to South Queensferry (Police Station) and walk west to Port Edgar (15 minutes). For a closer look, take bus X 54, X 55, X 58, X 59 or X 60 to the adjacent Forth Road Bridge – open to pedestrians as well as public transport | **Hours** Always accessible | **Tip** Port Edgar Marina offers coaching and taster sessions in a range of watersports, including windsurfing and paddleboarding, for adults and children. The harbour is also a nature conservation site, sheltering a variety of migratory seabirds including terns, which nest on an artificial floating island.

84 Torphichen Preceptory
Take the high road to Jerusalem

'Torphichen Preceptory' is a bit of a mouthful, frankly – a factor that probably contributes to the undeserved present-day obscurity of this fascinating relic. Things were clearly different in the Middle Ages, however, for the preceptory, or commandery, was then a place of far-reaching influence and renown. Founded around 1150 by King David I, the magisterial complex in the lee of the Torphichen Hills was no less than the sole Scottish base of the Knights Hospitaller, a wealthy international network of 'fighting monks' who came to prominence during the Crusades, that epic struggle between Christian and Muslim forces for dominion of the Holy Land.

Not to be confused with the Knights Templar, the Hospitallers, also known as the Order of St John, were a Christian brotherhood founded in Jerusalem in 1099 to care for the sick and needy. Soon after, their humanitarian role was extended to providing an armed escort for pilgrims undertaking the long, perilous journey to the Holy Land, and they acquired fortresses all over Europe. The Order later moved headquarters to Rhodes and finally to Malta, where their chivalric insignia of an eight-pointed cross became the island's well-known denominative emblem.

The surviving medieval block (now annexed to Torphichen's humbler parish kirk) is just a fragment of the Knights' original, hugely impressive church, which itself was only part of an extensive range of buildings that included cloisters, offices, living quarters and a farm. The elegant vaulted interior of the lofty bell tower still bears traces of painted decoration, while the atmospheric upper rooms house an absorbing exhibition on the history of the Order. The Hospitallers' 'Privilege' extended for a mile in each direction, an area within which criminals could claim immunity from prosecution. Four of the Sanctuary Stones that marked its limits survive, beyond the village.

Address Bowyett, Torphichen, EH48 4NB, +44 (0)1506 653733, www.historicenvironment.scot | **Getting there** Bus 31 to Torphichen | **Hours** Apr–Sept, Sat, Sun & Bank Holidays 1–5pm | **Tip** The village has a traditional local, the Torphichen Inn at 7 the Square, which deserves your custom. On your walk there, take time to explore the atmospheric kirkyard next door to the Preceptory. It has several vividly carved 18th-century gravestones, including a charming example to the rear of the church, where the naked figures of Adam and Eve are posed like highland dancers.

85 __ Binny Nursery

A garden is a lovesome thing

The horticultural phenomenon that is Binny Nursery basks in a pocket of tranquil rural seclusion within a landscape still tarnished by the shades of its industrial past. Established over 30 years ago by the charismatic Billy Carruthers, the five-acre plant business is based in and around the old kitchen garden of the long-dismantled Binny House Estate, sheltered within high buff sandstone walls on a south-facing slope.

Over the years, Binny has become a regular fixture in magazine lists of the UK's top retail nurseries, as well as a longtime prizewinner at the prestigious Chelsea Flower Show. Its specialisms are unusual perennials, trees, shrubs, ferns and grasses, all grown in peat-free soil; features include a willow tunnel, whose trimmings have supplied the appreciative giraffes at Edinburgh Zoo. It also hosts Scotland's National Bonsai Collection.

Though long acknowledged as one of Scotland's leading plantsmen, lecturers and garden designers, Billy had an unconventional journey to his vocation. After a spell in the rag trade, he moved into London's record business and established shops majoring in reggae music before the growing desire for a more peaceful life, centred on his childhood love of gardening, led him back to his native Scotland. When he first set up Binny Plants, Billy specialised in grasses – then considered avant-garde. But his lifetime passion is for peonies: he's keen to counter the common misconception that they're difficult to grow, and loves to share his extensive, experience-led knowledge. Binny's ever-expanding peony collection has now grown into one of the largest in the UK with over 300 varieties, from old cottage classics to a host of modern cultivars.

They have an excellent mail order service, but to appreciate the full range and beauty of what's on offer, as well as the special atmosphere of this lovely spot, a visit is essential.

Address Binny Estate, Ecclesmachan Road, Uphall, Broxburn, EH52 6NL, +44 (0)7753 626117, www.binnynurseries.com | **Getting there** Off B 8046 north of Uphall, on private road south-west of Ecclesmachan | **Hours** Daily 10am–5pm (Oct–Feb till 4pm); note that although there are toilets, there is no café or gift shop – this isn't that kind of garden centre | **Tip** Nearby Binny Craig is a prominent outcrop of igneous rock – a classic example of what geologists call a crag-and-tail formation – best accessed by a footpath from the minor road near East Broadlaw. A short but steep climb will take you to the summit and its panoramic views.

86__Five Sisters Zoo

The accidental animal sanctuary that just grew

Five Sisters must be the only accredited zoo in the world that began life as a garden centre. Back in 1993, landscape gardener Brian Curran and his wife Shirley bought a three-acre site to house their business, named after the massive bings (spoil heaps) that dominate West Calder. Both committed animal lovers, they also started taking in unwanted pets, which kept children entertained as their parents shopped. The garden centre soon began to fail, but the ever-growing animal community thrived, until in 2005 the couple applied for a licence to run a zoo, with the compassionate aim of operating chiefly as a rescue centre.

The collection of species was built up gradually, with meerkats, lemurs and exotic reptiles among popular early residents. Some creatures came from zoos with no space for them; others had been confiscated from smugglers or unscrupulous collectors. A new chapter opened in 2010, when the zoo gained a further tract of land, part of which was soon brought into use to rehabilitate three elderly bears, rescued from a European travelling circus. Always a hit with the local community, by 2012 Five Sisters had joined the ranks of the top 20 paying attractions in Scotland. A tragic setback came the following year when fire engulfed the reptile house, killing many species, but with the generous aid of supporters from around the world the Currans were soon able to rebuild and carry on.

Today, the zoo houses over 160 species. There are many that you could watch for hours, such as the irresistible prairie dogs, gregarious Corsac's foxes and delightful Humbolt's penguins, and if you're patient you'll see a variety of big cats, including snow leopards, ex-circus lions and a plucky three-legged cheetah. Two especially heart-warming stars are the brown bears, Eso and Byara, relishing life in their quiet two-acre woodland enclosure after being rescued from traumatic circumstances.

Address Polbeth Road, Gavieside, West Calder, EH55 8PT, +44 (0)1506 870000, www.fivesisterszoo.co.uk | Getting there Train to West Calder and a one-mile walk; bus 26 or 34a to Polbeth (Harwood Church) | Hours Daily Apr–Sept 10am–6pm, Feb, Mar & Oct 10am–5pm, Nov–Jan 10am–4pm | Tip A couple of miles west of the zoo is the abandoned toytown-castle curiosity that was once Freeport Village, an ambitious out-of-town retail and leisure complex. Opened in 1996 at the cost of £30 million, it closed just eight years later, and has since fallen into sad dereliction, though it has been used for civil defence exercises and a zombie-based reality TV show.

87 __ The Shale Trail

Stark legacy of Scotland's first oil boom

When is a hill not a hill? West Lothian folk should know the answer: when it's a bing. These man-made mini-mountains, otherwise known as spoil heaps, are the region's most prominent landmarks – vast pinkish-orange piles of discarded rock, created as the by-product of mining its rich reserves of oil-rich shale. Today, they stand as enigmatic memorials to the generations who toiled in the long-gone industry that transformed the rural landscape of West Lothian, along with the lives of its inhabitants.

It all began in 1850, when Scottish chemist James Young patented a process for extracting liquid fuel from seams of rock he discovered on the West Lothian coalfields. Just over a decade later he founded the world's first large-scale oil refinery, at Addiewell, launching a phenomenal boom that reached its peak in 1913, when three and a half million tons of the hard-won liquid were produced.

There are 19 bings scattered across West Lothian, the tallest rising 310 feet above the low-lying land. Abandoned when the mining era ended in the 1960s, they were seen at first as blots on the landscape, but in time local people came to view them with respect and even affection. Flora and fauna began to colonise their slopes, public art projects helped to rehabilitate their image, and several were designated as protected national monuments. Most recently, 2020 saw the inauguration of the Shale Trail, a 16-mile route for walkers and cyclists linking a series of the best-known bings including the iconic Five Sisters, which loom on the skyline near West Calder like the knuckles of a giant's fist. The bings themselves are quite safe to walk on, with tracks leading up through their otherwordly terrain to the summits. Along the trail, you can explore all the many aspects of the shale story by following the QR codes on the waymarker posts – everything from the primordial algae that generated the oily rocks to the Victorian country house that lies buried under one of those giant fingers.

Address Starts at Union Square, West Calder, EH55 8EY, and finishes at Winchburgh. For full details and an interactive map see www.shaletrail.co.uk | Getting there Train to West Calder, or Uphall (midway along the route). There are also bus links to several places on or near the trail | Hours Accessible 24 hours | Tip The Shale Trail website has a number of good resources for kids, including short videos narrated by local schoolchildren. There are also maps with suggested extensions to the route, leading to a variety of attractive green spaces and local places of interest.

88 Scottish Owl Centre
Memorable meetings with remarkable birds

Owls have a universal fascination that sets them apart from other birds. Part of this comes from their front-set, forward-facing eyes, an appealing feature that they share with our own species. Along with a catalogue of awe-inspiring abilities, such as soundless flight, astonishing night vision, ultra-sensitive hearing and a disconcerting facility for head rotation, this has given them a unique presence in our cultural history. There are over 250 types of owl in the world, but their elusive nature and largely nocturnal habits mean that seeing one in the wild is a rare event, becoming ever rarer as the ecological crisis takes its toll across the planet.

This is what makes a visit to the Scottish Owl Centre such an unforgettable privilege. With spacious aviaries enclosed in an old walled garden, it's home to around 150 owls, the largest collection in the world, from 50 different species of diverse beauty and charm. They range from the minute Pygmy to the majestic Eagle Owl, and include kinds you never knew existed – burrowing owls, fishing owls and a whole class that live in rainforests. Your amazement increases with each new encounter. Absolutely unmissable are the flying displays, where a select team of hand-reared owls show off their skills at close quarters, with engaging commentary from the highly knowledgeable keepers.

Ornithologist Rod Angus hatched this passion project in 2003 together with his wife Niccy, a former teacher who designs the excellent educational material and illuminating interpretation. Nine years later, they moved the growing venture from its original base in Argyll to the more accessible Polkemmet Country Park, to enable it to spread its wings, and its message. The ethos remains focused on education for all ages, with the aim of inspiring greater public interest in these wondrous birds, and in the pressing environmental issues that affect their survival in the wild.

Address Polkemmet Country Park, Whitburn, EH47 0AD, +44 (0)1501 228184, www.scottishowlcentre.com | **Getting there** Bus X18 to Polkemmet Road and a 15-minute walk; train to Shotts, then bus 23 to Polkemmet Country Park; by car, follow brown signs from M8 junction 4A | **Hours** Apr–Aug, daily 10.30am–5pm (Meet the Birds 11.30am, Flying Displays 1.30pm & 3.30pm), Feb, Mar, Sept, Oct, daily 11.30am–4pm (Flying Displays 12.30pm & 2.30pm), Jan & Nov, Sat & Sun 11.30am–2pm (Flying Display 12.30pm) | **Tip** Just across the courtyard from the entrance is the friendly Country Café, serving good-value hot drinks and snacks, including homemade soup.

89 Jupiter Artland
An evolving synthesis of art and landscape

It seems extraordinary, but there was no masterplan behind Jupiter Artland – in fact this phenomenal 120-acre sculpture park began life almost by accident. Its co-founders, Nicky and Robert Wilson, bought the estate on the western fringe of Edinburgh in 1999, along with the mansion at its centre, as a home for their young family, away from the constraints of life in London. The couple were avid art collectors, but several years passed before they had the notion of asking cultural theorist Charles Jencks to create a monumental landform within the grounds. The result, which he worked on from 2003 to 2010, was *Cells of Life*, a cluster of grassy mounds and shimmering ponds that wondrously celebrates the basic structure of all organisms. Jencks became a key influence as their idea took shape to fill the woodlands and meadows with site-specific sculptures and open it to the public, and it was he who suggested the name Artland, to evoke a place where art and landscape have equal status. The Wilsons added Jupiter, divine bringer of joy.

With almost 40 permanent installations now in place, the list of artists represented reads like what Nicky has described as a 'fantasy football team' of talent – Ian Hamilton Finlay, Anish Kapoor, Antony Gormley and Phyllida Barlow to name but a few. Each has produced a unique, personal response to the Artland environment, from Anya Gallaccio's *The Light Pours Out Of Me*, an amethyst-studded chamber that references the aristocratic follies of past centuries, to Jim Lambie's *A Forest*, whose peeling mirrored panels transform a steading building into a dreamlike extension of the woodland.

Educational outreach has been part of the Jupiter ethos from the start, with free visits offered to schools and colleges throughout Scotland, and a programme of temporary exhibitions means that there is always fresh creative expression on display.

Address Bonnington House Steadings, near Wilkieston, EH27 8BY, +44 (0)1506 889900, www.jupiterartland.org | **Getting there** Entrance on B 7105 west of Wilkieston (no access from Bonnington village), bus X 23 or X 27 to Coxydene / Jupiter Artland; book online for discount on entry ticket | **Hours** Apr – Sept daily 10am – 5pm (last entry 4pm) | **Tip** Jupiter has a dynamic programme of immersive activities, including wild swimming sessions within *Cells of Life*, bathing in Joana Vasconcelos' vibrantly tiled pool, *Gateway*, and creative woodland adventures for children aged three and upwards.

90__Callendar House

A magisterial venue for a fine local museum

Set in a vast expanse of pleasure grounds, the grandiose Callendar House is a conical-towered, mansard-roofed, three-storeyed château that wouldn't look out of place in the Loire Valley. It's an astonishing edifice to find in the heart of Scotland's industrial belt, just a short walk from the urban centre of Falkirk – made all the more exceptional by the fact that it's now a free-entry museum, filled with absorbing displays on the long and fascinating history of the house and sur-rounding district. Themes range from the medieval origins of Falkirk to its extraordinary transformation during the Industrial Revolution. You'll be introduced to some influential figures who have made this their residence, such as Sir Alexander Livingston, regent of Scotland in the mid-15th century, who appears in a striking lifesized funeral effigy, and Sir William Forbes, the *arriviste* copper merchant who bought the estate in 1783.

But the story really begins in the park, with the grassy mounds that flank the mansion's main entrance to impressive effect. These are remnants of the Antonine Wall, the Roman frontier built in the A.D. 140s, whose construction and impact on the area are vividly evoked in a display featuring a host of fascinating finds, among them a fine carving of Hercules from a relief on a nearby temple. Callendar House itself dates from the 14th century, when the estate was granted to the Livingston family, though their modest tower was subsumed long ago by subsequent enlargements and remod-elling, culminating in the 1870s with the Frenchified extravaganza that we see today.

There are plenty of splendid features from various periods to admire on your tour. Highlights include a *trompe l'oeil* Baroque ceiling painting with frolicking cherubs, a Georgian kitchen of surprising grandeur, and the luxuriously panelled 19th-century morning room, which now houses a popular café.

Address Callendar Road, Falkirk, FK1 1YR, +44 (0)1324 503772, www.falkirkleisureandculture.org | **Getting there** Train to Falkirk Grahamston or bus 2, 2A, 3, 4, 5, 7, 38, F 16 or X 38 to Falkirk town centre, then a 15-minute walk to the house from the High Street (signposted) | **Hours** Wed–Mon 10am–5pm | **Tip** The 'designed landscape' of Callendar Park was a private estate until 1963, but is now a fantastic public resource, much appreciated by the local community. Covering 170 acres, it includes extensive woodland with walking trails as well as ornamental gardens, a small loch and architectural curiosities such as the Neoclassical Forbes Mausoleum (sadly derelict). There's also a large children's play area, where a range of outdoor activities are available from April to September.

91__The Carron Clocktower

Lone relic of the ironheart that glows no more

Carron is a name that once resonated around the world. In 1759 a site by the river of that ilk was chosen by a trio of entrepreneurs for a pioneering iron foundry, the first and most influential of the 60 or so that flourished in the Falkirk area over the following 200 years. The Carron company quickly became a key player in the Industrial Revolution, and by 1810 it was the largest ironworks in Europe, with more than 2,000 employees. The glow from its blast furnaces used to light up the skyline for miles around.

All that remains of this colossus is a clocktower in Scots-Baronial style, built in the 1870s as the gateway to the redeveloped works, left as a token memorial after their demolition in 1990, and now looming in awkward isolation above a sea of industrial units and housing. Though semi-derelict and colonised by pigeons, the tower still bears vestiges of the company's former glory. A remnant of a steam condenser cast in 1766 for inventor James Watt is set into the stonework, while above the archway is Carron's phoenix crest, together with the hubristic motto *Esto perpetua* ('May it last for ever'). A plaque tells of early celebrity visitor Robert Burns, who was thwarted in his first attempt at a tour when he turned up on a Sunday. Within the portals is a display featuring the product that literally made the company's name – the carronade, a naval gun used to devastating effect in the Napoleonic Wars – plus two cannons that helped Wellington win Waterloo.

Armaments aside, it should be remembered that the Carron plant was also instrumental in transforming the living standards of millions, through its production of goods such as kitchen stoves and utensils, baths and drainage systems, not to mention postboxes and phone kiosks. It's even said that the origins of Scotland's favourite soft drink Irn Bru lie, fittingly, with the thirsty foundrymen of the Falkirk district.

Address Stenhouse Road, Carron, Falkirk, FK2 8FL | Getting there Bus 6, 6A, 7, 8 or F16 from Falkirk town centre to Burder Park | Hours Accessible 24 hours | Tip Falkirk Made Friends is a group formed in 2019 to promote the history of Ironheart – a collective name for the foundries of Falkirk district – and safeguard the surviving cast-iron phone boxes in the area. Among their achievements to date is the 49-foot-long Ironheart mural, painted in 2022 at the former Gowanbank Foundry, Gowan Avenue, and an Iron History Trail displayed on the phone box outside the Paterson Tower shop at Callendar Park.

92 The Falkirk Tunnel

The awe-inspiring outcome of 19th-century nimbyism

'The most perfect inland navigation between Edinburgh and Glasgow', the Union Canal was a state-of-the-art feat of engineering when it opened in 1822. Designed to link the capital with the existing Forth–Clyde canal at Falkirk, it had been a long time in the planning, with many different routes being considered before Hugh Baird's proposal was finally approved. His solution was a contour canal, following a meandering course at 240 feet above sea level, with river valleys bridged by elegantly engineered aqueducts.

But there was one snag that proved more obstructive than any natural feature. The Forbes family of Callendar House in Falkirk were incensed when they realised that the waterway would be visible from their estate, going so far as to commission two engravings showing 'before and after' views and sending copies to every MP in Britain. As a result, the plan was altered to incorporate a tunnel nearly half a mile long cut through solid rock, a backbreaking undertaking accomplished by squads of the tough manual labourers known as navigators, or navvies. Many of those who worked on the Union Canal project were Irish immigrants, including two men named Burke and Hare, later to gain notoriety as serial murderers who sold their victims' corpses to an Edinburgh surgeon for anatomical dissection.

An early guidebook to the canal describes the awe experienced by passengers gliding through the 'lonely dark arch' of the Falkirk Tunnel with 'their feelings... wound to the highest pitch'. Today, enhanced by colourful LED lighting, the cavernous passage is even more atmospheric for visitors both by boat and on foot, with the illumination picking out vivid evidence of its hard-won excavation – candle holders, dynamite stores and the marks of picks and shovels on the walls – as well as the beauty of the variegated mineral deposits and stalactites formed by two centuries of dripping water. The towpath can be slippery in places, but there is a reassuring handrail.

Address Union Canal, Falkirk, FK1 5LF | Getting there Train to Falkirk High; bus 7 or 8 to Drossie Road. The tunnel entrance is just behind Falkirk High Station | Hours Open 24 hours | Tip Once you emerge at the other end, take a walk a little further along the towpath to see the Laughin' and Greetin' Bridge, so called because of the contrasting faces carved on the keystones of its two sides. According to an old story, the one looking towards Falkirk is greeting (crying) in sympathy with the contractor tasked with cutting the tunnel and building the flight of 11 locks needed to reach the Forth–Clyde canal, while the laughing one looks out at the much more straightforward eastern section.

93 The Falkirk Wheel

Archimedes' principle still holds water – and how!

The list of facts and figures concerning the Falkirk Wheel is seriously impressive. The world's one and only rotating boat-lift, this 115-foot-tall, 1,800-tonne colossus is the lynchpin of a £20-million complex that includes a tunnel, aqueduct, canal extension and locks. It was completed in 2002 as the centrepiece of the Millennium Link, an imaginative regeneration scheme that transformed the whole 71-mile length of two long-neglected waterways, the Union and Forth–Clyde Canals, with the ambitious goal of reinstating a fully navigable route across central Scotland between Glasgow and Edinburgh. This meant connecting the canals at a site near Falkirk where the two were adjacent – but separated by a difference in height of 82 feet. The link was once provided by a flight of 11 locks that took the best part of a day to negotiate. Now, the ingenious Wheel allows boats to cover the distance in just five minutes, by simply (!) picking them up from one level and depositing them at the other.

Comprising two opposing arms, each of which holds a water-filled gondola capable of holding four boats, the lift is so finely balanced that it needs only minimal electricity, equivalent to that of boiling eight domestic kettles, to complete the required half turn. The key to the process is the age-old principle of fluid dynamics credited to Archimedes (of 'Eureka!' fame) – floating objects displace their own exact weight in water, so the load of 250 tonnes in each gondola remains the same, regardless of the number of boats being carried.

A ride on the Wheel is essential to experience the brilliance of its engineering and enjoy the sweeping vistas. But its elegant design can equally be appreciated from afar as a vast kinetic artwork. In the words of chief architect Tony Kettle, the effect of the slowly moving curves and reflections is kaleidoscopic, and mesmerising to watch.

Address Lime Road, Tamfourhill, FK1 4RS, +44 (0)300 3730868, www.scottishcanals.co.uk/falkirk-wheel | Getting there Train to Falkirk Grahamston, then bus 6 from Weir Street to Falkirk Wheel | Hours Visitor Centre open daily 9.45am–6pm; boat trips on the Wheel daily from 10am (check website for seasonal closing hours) | Tip The Wheelside basin hosts a range of fun activities for all ages, including canoeing, bumper boating, waterzorbing (walking on water inside a large bubble) and splashing across a huge stone map of Scotland. Bike hire and Segway tours of the surrounding area are also available for those who prefer dry land.

94 Inside the Kelpies
The complex anatomy of a pair of high horses

Scotland's most famous public sculpture has such an iconic status today that it's hard to believe it has only existed for a decade. The artwork in question is of course the Kelpies, the two 98-foot, 300-tonne, stainless steel horse heads that stand guard over a specially constructed lock on the Forth–Clyde canal as the crowning glory of Falkirk's Helix Park regeneration scheme. Though plaudits from the art world were notably lacking at their unveiling – the *Guardian* published a stinging diatribe that dismissed them as a 'pile of horse poo' – they were an immediate hit with the public, attracting international media attention and unforeseen streams of visitors, and making a household name out of sculptor Andy Scott.

Aesthetic differences aside, there was nothing but praise for the expertise of the engineers who translated Scott's scale models into gigantic reality – it took them eight years to overcome the structural challenges involved. The innovative solution they evolved depends on a complex internal framework in tubular steel to support the outer skin of 928 individually shaped panels; the result is a monumental abstract sculpture on its own terms, which can only be appreciated by touring the interior.

It was in fact an engineer, George Ballinger of British Waterways, who came up with the concept for the landmark, to honour the generations of heavy horses that once hauled barges on the canal and, more generally, the human-equine relationship that shaped our world for millennia. (He originally envisaged the two heads as functional, rocking backwards and forwards to operate the lock.) Ballinger was also responsible for their evocative if rather infelicitous name, which comes from Scots mythology. Like its namesakes, the legendary kelpie was a powerful equine creature, but a malevolent one – a shape-shifting aquatic spirit that appeared on the waterside in the form of a handsome horse, and lured passing humans to death by drowning.

Address The Helix, Falkirk, FK2 7ZT, +44 (0)1324 590600, www.thehelix.co.uk/visit/
kelpies-tour | Getting there Train to Falkirk Grahamston, then bus 2, 2A, 3, 4 or 28 from
Weir Street to Falkirk Stadium and a one-mile walk on signposted footpaths across Helix
Park | Hours Exterior: always accessible; Visitor Centre: daily 9am–5pm; tours of interior:
daily 10.30am, 11.30am, 1.30pm, 2.30pm & 3.30pm, bookable via website | Tip The
Charlotte Dundas Heritage Trail is a short, well-interpreted canalside walk that begins at
the Kelpies basin, celebrating 300 years of local history and in particular the story of the
world's first practical steamboat and its inventor, William Symington.

95 Rosebank Distillery
The fragrant return of the King of the Lowlands

Think of whisky and an image of a remote Highland glen probably comes to mind. Nonetheless, it was in the Lowlands that our native spirit was born (thanks to some convivial monks in medieval Fife, but that's another story) and the region became a designated area of production as long ago as 1784. By the end of the century there were no fewer than 31 Lowland distilleries in operation, including one by the Forth–Clyde canal at Camelon, near Falkirk. This was a prime location in an era when transporting goods by water was the most economic option, and in 1840 the same site was chosen by local grocer James Rankine for a distillery that he named Rosebank, after the flowers that grew on the waterside.

As is typical for Lowland malts, his product was triple distilled, and coal was used to fire the kilns. The result was a delightfully light, floral, unpeated dram of such high quality that it became one of the whiskies most favoured by blenders to give top notes to their liquor. By the 1880s it was being shipped to Australia, while nearer home Falkirk Parish Council voted to supply it to the inmates of a local poorhouse – for medicinal purposes, of course.

With its 108-foot chimney stack, the distillery was a distinctive Falkirk landmark as well as a valued employer. But a changing market led to its mothballing in 1993, to the dismay of connoisseurs who considered its single malt 'the King of the Lowlands'. Pigeons took up residence, and the stills were stolen by copper thieves. Then in 2017 the welcome news came that Rosebank was to be brought back into production under new owners.

Though the whisky isn't yet drinkable, the much-missed sweet aroma from the mash tuns, which locals liken to that of banana bread, pervades the area once again, and the beautifully refurbished building, which features a showpiece glass-fronted stillhouse and attractive visitor facilities, is now open for tours.

Address Camelon Road, Falkirk, FK1 5JR, +44 (0)1324 374100, www.rosebank.com | Getting there Train to Falkirk Grahamston or Camelon, then bus 1, 35, 38 or X37 Swift | Hours Daily: reception and shop, 10am–5.30pm; Rosebank Reawakening tours (90 minutes), 10.30am–3.45pm, time slots bookable online. See website for details of more specialist tours and tastings | Tip Take a short walk along the canalside opposite the distillery to admire the sculptures at Lock 2 – a striking group of monumental whisky bottles, outlined in Corten steel.

FALKIRK

96 Rough Castle
Romani ite domum – Romans go home!

Just a short walk from the Falkirk Wheel is another world-class marvel of engineering, albeit of a very different nature and era. The name 'Rough Castle' might suggest a craggy medieval bastion, but this is a much rarer survival – the well-preserved remains of a Roman fort at the final frontier of Britannia, the Antonine Wall.

Built in the A.D. 140s on the orders of Emperor Antoninus Pius, it superseded its big cousin Hadrian's Wall, 100 miles to the south, after the conquest of the intervening territory. Its 37-mile extent, from the Clyde to the Forth, may seem trifling for an empire whose bounds extended for over 3,100 miles. But its imposition was so fiercely challenged by the local tribes that it was the most complex of all Roman frontiers, with a massive ditch in front of a substantial wall of turf, earth and timber, laid on a stone base and punctuated by 17 forts and numerous look-out towers. Until the Industrial Revolution it remained the largest construction project ever undertaken in central Scotland. Still, Caledonia proved to be a bridge too far for the Romans: after only two decades the army withdrew back to Hadrian's Wall, and the new frontier was abandoned.

Rough Castle today is a tranquil and oddly beguiling spot. The remains of the military buildings were reburied after excavation, and time has mellowed the unbreachable earthworks into softly contoured grassy mounds and sheltered hollows. Only with the aid of the excellent information panels can you picture it as the base of Roman troops, battle-hardened warriors from the Nervii tribe of modern-day Belgium, commanded by a centurion of the 20th Legion named Gaius Flavius Betto. One vivid feature, however, stands out as a sharp reminder of its purpose: the rows of pits known as *lilia*, just beyond the north gate. These were originally camouflaged and furnished with wooden spikes to skewer the feet of would-be intruders – a passive defence that was the Roman equivalent of a minefield.

200

Address Antonine Wall, 1.25 miles east of Bonnybridge, Falkirk, FK4 2AA | Getting there Bus 6 to Falkirk Wheel, then follow signposted path from the Visitor Centre leading uphill and into community woodland (c.15 minutes) | Hours Accessible 24 hours | Tip Two other well-preserved remnants of the Wall can be seen nearby at Watling Lodge, Tamfourhill Road, where the ditch survives at close to its original dimensions, and at Anson Avenue, Bantaskin, where a section is marooned incongruously in the middle of a modern housing estate.

97 Blackness Castle

Dark bastion of war in ship-shape order

The stern, sea-girt castle of Blackness takes its name from the dark basalt rock that forms the promontory (or ness) on which it stands. But, in a parallel sense, the word is an apt descriptor for the austere fortress itself, with its sombre history of conflict and persecution. Most notoriously, it held within its walls a dreaded state prison. Some high rank captives enjoyed the relative luxury of confinement within the central tower, but others, notably the 17th-century religious and political dissenters known as the Covenanters, were held in Stygian dungeons that were flooded by the chilly waters of the Forth at each high tide.

The castle began life simply enough, as a residential tower house, built in the mid-15th century for the Admiral of Scotland, Sir George Crichton. A few years after its completion, however, it was appropriated as crown property by the bellicose James II, who no doubt coveted its strategic coastal location. Under successive monarchs, it was remodelled and increasingly fortified, and by the 1540s it had become a virtually impregnable garrisoned stronghold, incorporating a forbidding prison for enemies of the state, in use for centuries. In the 1870s its military career entered a new phase when it was converted into an ammunition depot, with a cast-iron jetty to facilitate deliveries.

A distinctive feature of the 16th-century fortifications is the layout of the curtain wall and towers: when viewed from the seaward side, particularly downriver, these give the castle the aspect of a great stone warship, complete with prow, stern and main mast.

Be sure to take a walk around the ramparts and enjoy the commanding views over the Firth of Forth. You'll be following in the footsteps of the young Mel Gibson, who played the gloomy Dane in Franco Zeffirelli's *Hamlet*, shot here in 1989 when stellar productions filmed in Scotland were a rarity.

Address Blackness, EH49 7NH, +44 (0)1506 834807, www.historicenvironment.scot | Getting there Bus F 49 from Linlithgow or Bo'ness | Hours Daily, Apr–Sept 9.30am–5pm, Oct–Mar 10am–4pm | Tip The Lobster Pot in nearby Blackness village is a bright and welcoming pub/tearoom, with a menu that (unsurprisingly) includes lobster. It also houses the village shop.

98_Bo'ness & Kinneil Railway

Right on track for a nostalgic day out

Steam trains have a special place in Britain's history. The world's first public railway opened here in 1825, and within two decades locomotives had puffed, clanked and hissed their way into the very fabric of the nation, maintaining their supremacy up to the 1930s. But the decline of the railways during wartime led to their nationalisation in 1948, and modernisation soon followed.

As the old engines were phased out in favour of diesel, groups of enthusiasts got together all over the UK, dedicated to preserving vintage trains and running them as leisure attractions. One of these was the Scottish Railway Preservation Society, formed in 1961 with the goal of establishing their own heritage railway. Finally, in 1979, they settled on a greenfield site at Bo'ness and began transforming it into a home for their growing collection of rail vehicles and equipment.

It's truly astounding to see what this voluntary organisation has achieved since then. There's a historically authentic station, amassed chiefly out of stylish Victorian buildings rescued from around central Scotland, and operated by appropriately uniformed staff. There's a vast and utterly absorbing museum telling the story of Scottish railways, filled with a huge range of lovingly restored rolling stock (including a travelling Post Office) and artefacts from station signs to rule books. But best of all is the chance of an outing by steam train, a scenic 10-mile round trip, through Kinneil and the bijou station at Birkhill, then over the Avon viaduct to the terminus at Manuel (whose name derives from the nearby medieval nunnery of Emmanuel). It's a leisurely, immersive adventure for all the senses as well as a celebration of important industrial heritage, evoking nostalgia for a lost era that we all love to view through the romantic lens of *The Railway Children*, *Brief Encounter* and the like.

Address Bo'ness Station, Union Street, Bo'ness, EH51 9AQ, +44 (0)1506 825855, www.bkrailway.co.uk | **Getting there** Bus 2, 2A, F45 or F49 to Bo'ness Main Street, or 909 (Citylink) to Gauze Road and a 15-minute walk | **Hours** Train trips: Easter–Oct & Dec, Sat & Sun plus midweek during school holidays; see website for timetable; Museum: Easter–Oct & event days in Dec, daily 11am–4.30pm | **Tip** For many years two vintage coaches at the station have housed a model railway display depicting the scenic 'Glenauchter', designed, constructed and operated by enthusiasts of the Bo'ness Gauge O Group. In May 2024 this delightful creation was badly damaged by a mindless arson attack; however, after a successful fundraising appeal the group are now working hard to restore and rebuild the much-loved attraction.

99__Bo'ness Motor Museum

From Bond to Buddhism, via Potter and Trotter

Its laconic name might suggest that it's strictly for petrolheads, but there's a whole lot more to this enjoyably quirky museum than the anticipated rows of gas-guzzling automobiles. While the core collection is indeed classic cars, the focus is chiefly on vehicles that have featured in film and TV, plus associated ephemera, particularly from James Bond and space fiction movies, and the labyrinthine displays are jam-packed with an absorbing miscellany of memorabilia and props. You'll find everything from a replica Golden Gun to a seven-foot Starship *Enterprise*, along with plenty of video clips showing 007's automotive co-stars in nail-biting action.

Private motor museums have a notoriously high closure rate, and it's a credit to proprietor Colin Anderson that his eclectic creation is still drawing appreciative visitors 20 years after its opening. A businessman with a background in the antiques trade, he had bought the derelict building with demolition in mind, when a meeting with an enterprising car museum owner made him see the potential of using it to put his own growing collection of vehicles on display to the public. As the home of Scotland's earliest motor-racing fixture, the Bo'ness Hill Climb, the town seemed an appropriate site. The Bond theme began to proliferate after Colin acquired the museum's signature car: a 1976 Lotus Esprit S 1, used in *The Spy who Loved Me* by his favourite 007, Roger Moore.

Other popular favourites as seen on small and big screen range from Del Boy Trotter's Reliant Regal to the 'flying' Ford Anglia from *Harry Potter and the Chamber of Secrets*. But for fans of curiosities from real life (or real death…) the most jaw-dropping exhibit must be the Japanese hearse, modified to resemble a mini-Buddhist temple, complete with ornate brass fittings and extravagant gilded carvings incorporating dragon, peacock and lion motifs.

Address Bridgeness Road, Bo'ness, EH51 9JR, +44 (0)1506 827007, www.motor-museum.bo-ness.org.uk | **Getting there** Bus 2, 2A, F45 or F49 to Philpingstone Road, or Citylink 909 and a 0.6 mile walk (steep hill) | **Hours** Sat & Sun 11am–4pm (last admission). Phone to check in winter months. Weekdays open by appointment for groups | **Tip** Another intriguing collection for transport enthusiasts is Myreton Motor Museum, hidden away in rural East Lothian, near Aberlady. Founded in 1966 by local farmer Willie Dale and now run by his family, it features cars of all periods including vintage, as well as motorcycles and extensive motoring memorabilia.

100_ The Bridgeness Slab
Cultural restitution in Bo'ness

One of the finest pieces of Roman sculpture ever found in Britain is the ornate stone tablet unearthed near Bridgeness Tower in April 1868. The well-preserved nine-foot slab was soon identified as part of the Antonine Wall, the frontier built in the A.D. 140s at the northern limit of the Roman Empire, whose easternmost end lay nearby. The legionaries who constructed it were skilled craftsmen as well as trained soldiers, and to show their pride in their work they erected a series of 'distance slabs' – unique in the Roman world – at intervals along its 37-mile length. Of the 20 that have been found, the Bridgeness Slab is the most impressive. Its inscription, recording the completion of a four-mile stretch by the Second Legion, is flanked by vivid high-relief carvings of a dedication ceremony with animal sacrifice, and a cavalryman subduing hapless local tribesmen. These were originally brightly painted; details such as the red blood on a severed human head would no doubt have added to their impact.

Recognising its significance, the landowner presented it to the National Museum of Antiquities in Edinburgh, who erected a modest plaque near the find spot. Then in 2002 a Bo'ness councillor intent on raising the profile of the town's Roman history began a campaign for the slab's restitution to its rightful home. The Museum rejected the request, but supported the idea of creating a full-sized replica. This could not be made by moulding and casting, due to the fragility of the surface, but a process using 3-D scanning technology was developed to guide a team of masons who carved an exact copy in sandstone.

The magnificent result was finally unveiled in 2012 on an open-air site by the line of the wall, to justifiable acclaim by the local community. The ghosts of the Second Legion must surely be tickled pink by such a generous accolade from these latter-day friendly natives.

Address Kinningars Park, Harbour Road, Bo'ness, EH51 9LF | Getting there Bus 45, 46 or F45 to Bo'ness (Victoria Mills) | Hours Accessible 24 hours | Tip The park was once part of the estate of the long-gone Grange House – the name Kinningars (Scots for 'warren') shows that it was used for breeding rabbits for their table. Across the grass is a dovecot with 415 nesting boxes that provided pigeons for a later incarnation of the house. This was, unusually, converted from an 18th-century winding-engine house that served a nearby coal mine.

101 The Hippodrome
Reviving the magic of the silver screen

In a world where instant access to countless streams of moving images is an unremarkable feature of everyday life, it's difficult to imagine how much the treat of 'going to the pictures' meant to former generations, particularly the awe-struck audiences of the silent era. But there is one unexpected location that offers a precious window on to this lost world: the historic burgh of Bo'ness, home of Scotland's oldest surviving purpose-built cinema, the Hippodrome, originally opened in 1912 and reborn some 97 years later after being rescued from decades of dereliction.

Moving pictures came early to Bo'ness, with a film show in the Drill Hall in 1897 – just two years after the Parisian public first thrilled to the Lumière Brothers' astonishing invention. The fact that the Forthside town remained at the forefront of the new entertainment sensation was down to two inspirational local figures, electrician turned cinematographer Louis Dickson, and Matthew Steele, the visionary architect he commissioned to create the stylish picture palace, with its distinctive round auditorium.

Beautifully restored in star-spangled, sunburst splendour, and revamped with 21st-century technology, the Hippodrome is now a modern movie theatre for the local community, screening new releases, family films and arthouse fare as well as hosting events and private parties. But its greatest pride and joy is Hippfest, Scotland's only festival dedicated to silent film. Running annually since 2011, it features many rare gems, all shown with live musical accompaniment and complemented by talks and workshops. Every March, expert enthusiasts and curious neophytes alike flock from far and near to revel in the lovingly curated programme, and in a nostalgic nod to a fondly remembered custom, there's always one screening where a clean, empty jeely (jam) jar will gain you entry in lieu of a ticket.

Address 10 Hope Street, Bo'ness, EH51 0AA, +44 (0)1324 506850, www.hippodromecinema.co.uk | Getting there Bus 2, F 45 or Citylink 909; shuttle bus service from Linlithgow Station during Hippfest (booking essential) | Hours Daily; see website for programme | Tip Bo'ness also possesses a bijou community theatre, the Barony, home to the long-established Barony Players, who present a varied programme of drama throughout the year in its 120-seat auditorium.

102 James Watt's Workshop
Full steam ahead into the future

The formidable 17th-century mansion of the Dukes of Hamilton is now an empty shell, yet it still dominates the estate of Kinneil, and it's easy to miss the tiny cottage that sits to its rear. The modesty of this humble, roofless ruin belies its historical magnitude: though later converted into a washhouse, it was originally constructed in 1768 as a secret workshop for inventor James Watt, to enable him to conduct experiments on a new steam engine. The success of his design proved to be a true game-changer – the spark that lit the touch paper of the Industrial Revolution, forever altering the course of history.

The popular tale of young Jamie musing beside a boiling kettle has led to the erroneous belief that he was the first person ever to harness the power of steam. In fact, Thomas Newcomen's 'atmospheric engine', invented in 1712, was widely used for decades to pump water out of mines, although it was highly inefficient and hugely wasteful of energy. In May 1765 the ingenious Watt realised that the key to improving the Newcomen engine was to introduce a separate condensing chamber. His lightbulb moment (to use a happy anachronism) came to him not in his mother's kitchen, but as he was crossing Glasgow Green.

Kinneil House was at that time leased to pioneering industrialist Dr John Roebuck, who was keen to exploit the area's coal reserves. But draining the pits was a major problem, and on hearing that Watt was working on an idea for a new and better engine, Roebuck offered to sponsor him in constructing a prototype, in return for a share of the patent. Watt chose a site for his workshop that offered seclusion as well as a plentiful supply of water, and so, for a brief period, this quiet spot by the Gil Burn was transformed into the most important place in the world. A condenser from Watt's earliest steam engine serves as a stolid and unpretentious monument.

Address Kinneil Estate, Provost Road, Bo'ness, EH51 0PJ, www.kinneil.org | **Getting there** Bus 45, 46 to Kinneil House or bus 909 to Bo'ness (Livingstone Drive); Workshop signposted from the exit in the wall just to the left of Kinneil House | **Hours** Accessible 24 hours | **Tip** Though mostly gutted, Kinneil House boasts a series of 16th- and 17th-century wall paintings that are among the finest surviving in Scotland, including figurative scenes by a European artist trained in tapestry design. Visits are restricted to a few Open Days per year.

103___Kinneil

Vanished village at the head of the wall

The bucolic peace of the parkland at Kinneil, on the western edge of Bo'ness, masks a long and eventful history of human activity. Tantalising hints of those who once trod this ground are dotted all around its lush meadows and woods, including the remains of a fortlet from the Antonine Wall that housed Roman troops during their brief Caledonian incursion. But the most poignant relic is the scant evidence of the numerous generations who made this place their home in later centuries, in the village that was obliterated.

Kinneil means 'wall's end' (though in fact that extended further east), and it's one of the oldest recorded Scottish place names. Traditionally linked to the 6th-century missionary St Serf, the site was settled in early Christian times by a community of monks. The village grew up in the feudal era, under the protection of the laird whose tower stood across the Gil Burn, and in the 12th century a sturdy parish church was erected for its people. By the 17th century Kinneil had become a 'considerable town', counting many skilled tradesmen among its population.

But times were changing. The laird's residence was now a fine palace, and in the 1660s the estate's ancestral owners, the Hamilton family, decided to improve it further by creating a fashionable designed landscape. The townsfolk were 'encouraged' to move to the emerging port of Bo'ness, as their homes were pulled down to make way for pleasure grounds and a 'gallop' for the Duke's horses. Their ancient church was 'supressed'; in his final sermon, the minister cursed the Hamiltons, threatening vengeance on anyone who tried to demolish it. And so the building was retained for their private use (and paved with reused gravestones) until it was accidentally destroyed by fire in 1745. One solitary, defiant gable survives, now accompanied by a sympathetic memorial in weathered steel.

Address Kinneil Estate, Provost Road, Bo'ness, EH51 0PJ, www.kinneil.org | Getting there Bus 45 or 46 to Kinneil House, or bus 909 to Bo'ness (Livingstone Drive) | Hours Accessible 24 hours | Tip Housed in a former stable block, the excellent Kinneil Museum gives a comprehensive account of the estate's history, with fascinating exhibits including many Roman finds (Wed–Mon 12.30–4pm). Oh – and look out for the ghost who allegedly haunts the area near the burn, said to be that of a certain Lady Lilbourne, the unhappy wife of a Cromwellian general who threw herself from a top-floor window of the house.

104 Bonnymuir Memorial

'Say not the struggle naught availeth'

The bloody clash at Culloden that ended the Jacobite Rising in 1746 is always said to be the last battle fought on British soil. But there is a much later contender for that grim credit: the ignominious rout by crack government troops of a small band of ill-armed artisans that took place on moorland near Bonnybridge on 5 April, 1820, during the 'Radical War'. Woefully little-remembered today, this was a turbulent week of strikes, riots and violent protests across central Scotland, the culmination of years of frustrated campaigning by exploited and increasingly impoverished workers demanding social justice and parliamentary reform.

The radicals who fought that day were handloom weavers from Glasgow and Condorrat, on their way to Falkirk, where they planned to join up with a group of nail makers in Camelon before seizing armaments from Carron Iron Works. But their ranks had been infiltrated by government informers – the weavers were intercepted at Bonnymuir by sabre-wielding cavalry and overwhelmed after a brief skirmish. Though no one died in the fighting, the 'Scottish Insurrection' was crushed. The leaders, John Baird and Andrew Hardie, were condemned to a death reserved for traitors – hanging followed by decapitation – and 19 other men and boys were deported to penal colonies in Australia. It would be 12 more years before the transformation of the electoral system began with the passing of the Great Reform Act, which paved the way for the voting rights that we now take for granted.

Two simple but moving monuments mark the battle site, the first erected in 2007 by the 1820 Society, an organisation committed to ensuring that the Radical War is not forgotten, and the second commissioned by Falkirk Council to mark the bicentenary in 2020. Sadly, the ceremony planned for its dedication was cancelled due to the Covid pandemic.

Address Broomhill Road (B 816), High Bonnybridge, FK4 2BD | **Getting there** On B 816 east of High Bonnybridge, just beyond a group of industrial units to the south of the road | **Tip** The route taken by the captured weavers as they were marched to jail in Stirling passes under the Forth–Clyde canal at Bonnybridge via a tunnel built in the late 1780s, said to be the earliest surviving in Scotland. In April 1981 it was named the Radical Pend, and a commemorative plaque erected after a pageant organised by Billy Buchanan, later a local councillor and provost.

105__ Seabegs Wood

The extraordinary legacy of alien invaders

Despite its status as a World Heritage Site, the Antonine Wall has a strangely low profile as a visitor attraction. Built in the A.D. 140s to establish the control of Roman emperor Antoninus Pius over a newly won tract of northern Britannia, it stretched from coast to coast right across the narrow waist of Scotland, forming a highly visible and heavily garrisoned barrier that imposed a powerful new order on the populace and the landscape they inhabited. It was quite simply one of the most awe-inspiring structures that this country has ever known.

Rather than a wall as we now understand the term, the *Vallum Antonini* was a complex affair made up of a series of interrelated features – a ditch up to 15 feet deep, an outer mound and a metalled road, as well as a 10-foot-high rampart. This was constructed largely from turf, a tough and effective material, albeit associated these days more with leisure pursuits than military engineering projects. (It's estimated that the quantity used was enough for 62 football pitches.) But less than a decade after the colossal undertaking was completed, the Romans retreated and their impregnable frontier was abandoned. Its looming presence was gradually softened by weathering, and its alien builders were forgotten.

One of its most evocative remnants can be seen in the pleasant woodland at Seabegs, where a quarter-mile stretch survives complete with a section of the military way, part of a network of roads that ultimately led to Rome. As you walk in the footsteps of the legionaries, you can't help noticing that three more modern east-west transport routes are all running alongside – a road, a railway and the Forth–Clyde canal. They're an apt reminder of the permanent impact that the Wall's construction had on the Scottish landscape, and of the immense expertise of the Roman surveyors and engineers who mapped out its course.

Address Near Bonnybridge, nearest postcode FK4 2BY; www.antoninewall.org | Getting there On B 816, one mile west of Bonnybridge; bus X 37 to Allandale, then a 20-minute walk east along the Forth–Clyde Canal towpath and under the canal via the Doctor's Pend | Tip One mile west of Seabegs, Allandale is a 'model' village whose layout exactly follows the course of the Wall. Built between 1904 and 1928 as housing for employees of local firebrick manufacturer J. G. Stein, it consists of two long rows of attractive workers' cottages, with front gardens and rear drying greens. All were furnished with inside toilets and baths, plus (even more unusually) electricity from 5am to 11pm.

106_ The Dunmore Pineapple
The apotheosis of King Pine

Dismiss all thoughts of syrupy chunks and deplorable pizzas. The gargantuan pineapple that tops the garden pavilion at Dunmore Park is of a wholly superior order, created in an era when it was a highly prized commodity that few in Britain had ever tasted. Originally painted in realistic colours, the 46-foot *tour de force* of stone carving was commissioned around 1777 by John Murray, 4th Earl of Dunmore, as a finishing touch for his walled garden, where the tropical fruit was grown – at huge trouble and astronomical expense – in hothouse 'pineries'.

Though it now looks so quirkily original, Murray's conspicuous expression of one-upmanship was absolutely in line with the fashion of his day. Throughout the Georgian era, the gentry of Britain and its North American colonies were gripped by a veritable pineapple mania, and its prestigious shape graced every kind of grand decorative context, from the giant finials on the towers of St Paul's Cathedral to aristocratic gateposts and railings, tea-sets and tombs.

The exotic fruit, named for its resemblance to the pine cone, had been an object of fascination in the West since Columbus first brought a specimen back from Guadeloupe in 1493. Its spiky crown and armoured body (with Fibonacci-sequenced fruitlets) led to its glorification as 'King Pine', and it acquired further cultural symbolism as the colonisation of the New World progressed. The British craze began when George I was served one of the very first home-grown pineapples, cultivated at Richmond in 1716. Though their cost was prohibitive – equivalent to that of a coach – they soon became a must-have centrepiece at top dinner parties. Wannabees unable to afford their own could rent a wilting fruit for the day (but not eat it).

No one nowadays would dream of renting a pineapple, of course – except this very special one, which is let out as totally unique holiday accommodation.

Address Dunmore Park, Airth, FK2 8LU, nts.org.uk/visit/places/the-pineapple | **Getting there** Bus F 16 to Dunmore Road End; follow signposted footpath for about one mile from bus stop, turning left at the first junction along a lovely tree-lined avenue | **Hours** Accessible 24 hours (viewable from the outside only). To rent the Pineapple (sleeps four) for a holiday, see landmarktrust.org.uk | **Tip** The Tudor-Gothic style mansion house of Dunmore Park is now a romantic ruin, half-hidden in the well-wooded grounds. Just across the A 905 is the model village of Dunmore, a quiet community of charming cottages in vernacular styles set round a village green, part of which is now a sensory garden.

107 __ The Grangemouth Mosaic

Unsung art treasure by two brilliant mavericks

The 1970s shopping precinct that dominates the centre of Grangemouth was planned with rather more sensitivity than most of Scotland's modernist malls, incorporating leafy outdoor seating areas with decorative paving and airy, green-liveried arcades that mirror the layout of the old streets they replaced. Five decades on, it seems in surprisingly good shape, boasting rarities like a proper fishmonger and an enterprising craft studio alongside the usual budget stores. But the indisputable jewel in its crown is the public artwork that was literally embedded into the development in 1975 – a mural of such stunning quality that it should long ago have been designated a National Treasure.

The Grangemouth Mosaic was the result of a felicitous collaboration between two of the most individualistic Scottish artists of the 20th century, Alan Davie and George Garson. Davie was a native of the town, born in 1920; he travelled widely, first on a life-changing student scholarship and then throughout his long career, achieving worldwide recognition for his colourful abstract paintings with their highly personal language of esoteric symbolism. Garson was a blunt-spoken former shipyard worker whose rare talent as a mosaicist was recognised when he attended Edinburgh College of Art in the 1960s as a mature student, and who went on to develop the technique into a creative art form of his own. It's a tribute to his expressive skills that he succeeded in conveying both the vibrancy and the painterly energy of Davie's design in his handling of the countless tiny *smalti* – hand-cut chunks of glass coloured with metal oxides – that make up the image. Set high on the drab wall of what was originally a two-storey department store, its shimmering colours and haunting atavistic motifs refuse to submit to the shouty, garish fascia of the charity shop that now occupies the space beneath.

Address York Square, Grangemouth, FK3 8BB | Getting there Bus 2, 3 or 4 to La Porte Precinct, or Citylink 909 to Beancross Road and one-mile walk | Hours Accessible 24 hours | Tip Grangemouth was once home to the vast but short-lived Central Scotland Airport, which became a state-of-the-art training centre for pilots during World War II. The Spitfire Memorial is a full-sized replica aircraft, unveiled in 2013 on the site of the airfield as a moving tribute to the 71 young men, from Poland and other nations, who lost their lives here while learning to manoeuvre the famous fighter plane.

108 Jupiter Urban Wildlife

Making space for nature to revive

With a history of oil refining that goes back a century, the town of Grangemouth is synonymous with petrochemicals, although its days as a centre of production are now numbered. Its cooling towers, furnaces and flare stacks, visible for miles around, are an undeniably awesome sight, if hard to reconcile with a historic description of the original Forthside port as a 'Venice of the north'. Long since demolished, it was one of Scotland's earliest planned towns, founded in 1772 as the eastern terminus of the Forth–Clyde canal, with a flat, low-lying hinterland that aided its subsequent exponential growth as a centre of trade and industry.

All this development came, of course, at an environmental cost, but in 1989 the chemical giant ICI contacted the Scottish Wildlife Trust (SWT) to discuss giving something back, by leasing them a four-hectare pocket of wasteland (once home to a dye works, and later a railway siding) to be redeveloped as a nature conservation area. Adopting the catchy name of the former cash and carry warehouse on the edge of the reserve that was commandeered to provide a base for its project workers, Jupiter Urban Wildlife Centre opened to the public in 1992.

With a patchwork of varied habitats including ponds, flower-rich meadows and a wild wood, all supporting a wealth of biodiversity, Jupiter is a remarkable testament to the potential of nature to recover and regenerate itself, even in the most unpromising setting. The trees, thickets, grassland and wetland are alive with multiple species of insects, birds and amphibians, providing a truly inspirational family-friendly resource for visitors of all ages.

In September 2023 the SWT, whose rangers had managed the site and organised educational activities for 30 years, announced that they were pulling out. But Jupiter isn't going anywhere, and local conservation organisations plan to reopen it as a community asset.

Address Wood Street, Grangemouth, FK3 8LH | **Getting there** Citylink bus 909 or First Bus 4 to Beancross Road, then follow signposts | **Hours** See www.scottishwildlifetrust/consultation/for current information | **Tip** The recently regenerated Zetland Park is Grangemouth's other green oasis, an 18.5 hectare open space in the heart of town with a fine rose garden as well as amenities including tennis courts and children's play areas. Look out for the graphic war memorial by John James Burnet, unveiled in 1923, which features a lion representing the British Empire devouring the stricken eagle of Germany.

109__ Tor Wood

A singular tower and a mystifying pool

The folk legends of our collective memory are rich in tales of the wildwood – mysterious forests filled with hidden secrets – so it can be easy for your mind to slip into this realm as you explore Tor Wood, a history-steeped enclave that was part of the medieval Royal Forest. You may not find a gingerbread house or an enchanted palace, but it does conceal two tantalising structures of obscure origins, well worth seeking out amid the trees. Though separated by many centuries, both are, coincidentally, circular in plan, which seems to add to their fascination.

Near the summit of a rocky slope is Tappoch Broch, a massive ruined tower 80 feet in diameter and probably over 2,000 years old. In summer it's so well camouflaged by undergrowth that coming upon it is not unlike discovering the remains of a Mayan citadel in the Guatemalan rainforest. Brochs – a uniquely Scottish phenomenon – are tall, windowless dwellings of great structural complexity, accessed by stairs within their hollow drystone walls. Built throughout the Iron Age, they combine elements of fortified house, fort and status symbol, but their exact function is unclear. Around 570 broch sites are known, almost all in the north and west of the country, so this Lowland outlier is a rarity.

Another part of the wood shields an entirely different curiosity: the Blue Pool. Apparently plonked in the middle of nowhere, this is a brick-lined hollow 20 feet across and 12 feet deep, filled with water of a strange turquoise hue. Of all the theories that have been put forward to explain its purpose, the most likely is that it was originally part of an air shaft serving the Quarter Colliery, a nearby pit, closed in 1910 and now flooded. The water's colour (which is less vivid than it used to be) may come from aluminium sulphate seeping from fireclay underlying the coal seam. But some people have other ideas, both prosaic and outlandish.

Address Torwood, Larbert, FK5 4SW | Getting there Bus 38 to Torwood Village (Glen Road). From Glen Road walk up Castle Loan towards Torwood Castle. At the junction near the castle entrance take the track leading right until you reach a crossroads. Tappoch Broch is signposted to the right; for the Blue Pool, go through the gate on the left and follow the path along the edge of the wood (signposted to Denny) for about half a mile until you come to a clearing and a line of electricity pylons. The pool is just beyond the gap in the wall | Tip Torwood Castle, once the seat of the Forrester clan, is an impressive 16th-century ruin with a complicated recent history of attempts at restoration. Gary Grant, a local enthusiast who has become its unofficial keeper, is often on site and welcomes visitors.

110__ Westquarter Dovecot

Bijou historic residence for birds

Less than two miles east of Falkirk town centre stands a 1930s council estate that was described in its day as 'the most important development in the history of Scottish housing'. Built to rehouse mining families living in appalling slums, Westquarter is an Arts-and-Crafts-style model village, with spacious cottages set in greenery around a wooded glen. In previous centuries this land was part of 300 landscaped acres belonging to the Livingston family; their ancestral mansion is no more, but one intriguing landmark survives as a reminder of their long-gone lifestyle – an 18th-century dovecot (pigeon house), lined on the interior with 868 nesting boxes.

Known in Scotland as doocots, these structures are a curious cultural phenomenon. A widespread feature of the Scottish rural scene from the 16th to the early 19th century, they were built by the landed gentry to provide a convenient source of meat, though they were unpopular with tenant farmers, whose fields were often ravaged by the laird's foraging pigeons. The guano from the doocot floor was also highly valued, above all as a fertiliser, vital for the fecund walled gardens of the nobility. As doocots developed as status symbols, so their architecture evolved, from round 'beehive' towers to the rectangular 'lectern' style, of which Westquarter Dovecot is a well-preserved and unusually ornate example. The south-facing lean-to roof and crow-stepped gables gave the birds sheltered places to perch.

Doocots were protected by both law and superstition, and hundreds survive to this day across central Scotland. In 1948 there was a move to have Westquarter's demolished, with councillors arguing that it was a relic of 'evil times', best forgotten. Fortunately, preservationists thought otherwise, and in 1950 it was taken into state care, complete with a neat privet hedge in homage to its present-day surroundings.

Address Dovecot Road, Westquarter, FK2 9YT | Getting there Bus 1 from Falkirk town centre | Hours Accessible 24 hours (viewable from the outside only) | Tip The adjacent Westquarter Glen is a wonderful public park, with picturesque woodland walks along the banks of a cascading burn, in a designed landscape that has remained largely unchanged since the 17th century.

111_ The John Muir Way

Happy trails!

Pioneer environmentalist, political campaigner, philosopher – John Muir was all of these things and many more. At heart, however, he was a rambler who loved nothing more than walking: when asked at the age of 74 to define his occupation, he answered 'Tramp'. In his adoptive USA, where he is lauded as the Father of the National Parks, a long-distance trail named in his honour was established soon after his death in 1914. But it was not till a century later that the land of his birth followed suit, with the inauguration of Scotland's own John Muir Way, a 134-mile walking route across the Central Belt from Helensburgh on the Firth of Clyde, where he set sail for America as a boy, to his birthplace by the North Sea coast in Dunbar. Covering a huge variety of terrain – rolling farmland, canalside townscapes, country parks and coastal clifftops – it's divided into 10 sections, making it easy to tackle as a series of day walks. There are public transport links along most of the way, and the website has interactive maps and other information to help you plan your outing.

About two thirds of the trail falls within the territory covered by this book, from Section 4, which enters Falkirk District just west of Allandale on the Forth – Clyde Canal towpath, to Section 10, the final stage, which ends at Muir's Birthplace Museum in Dunbar. Highlights *en route* include many of the 110 places described in the preceding pages, sites as varied as Seabegs Wood, the Falkirk Wheel, Callander House, Bo'ness & Kinneil Railway, Blackness Castle, Prestongrange Museum and Yellowcraig Beach.

It's a landscape shaped and forever changed by millennia of human activity, in contrast to the remote, unspoilt nature that Muir so fervently espoused. Nonetheless, he would surely have approved of the mission in his name to encourage his countryfolk to get out and enjoy the simple act of walking.

Address For full details of route see www.johnmuirway.org. Sections 4 to 10, from Allandale in Falkirk District to Dunbar in East Lothian, come within the scope of this book | **Getting there** Buses and trains serve numerous places along the route | **Tip** The John Muir Link is an additional eastward section of waymarked paths that lead along the East Lothian coast beyond Dunbar as far as Dunglass, on the border with Berwickshire. It's a varied 10-mile route that takes you close to a number of sights including Barns Ness Lighthouse (whose cottage is let as holiday accommodation), Torness Power Station (ch. 44), a natural sea arch at Bilsdean and, at the end, an idyllically sited medieval chapel, Dunglass Collegiate Church.

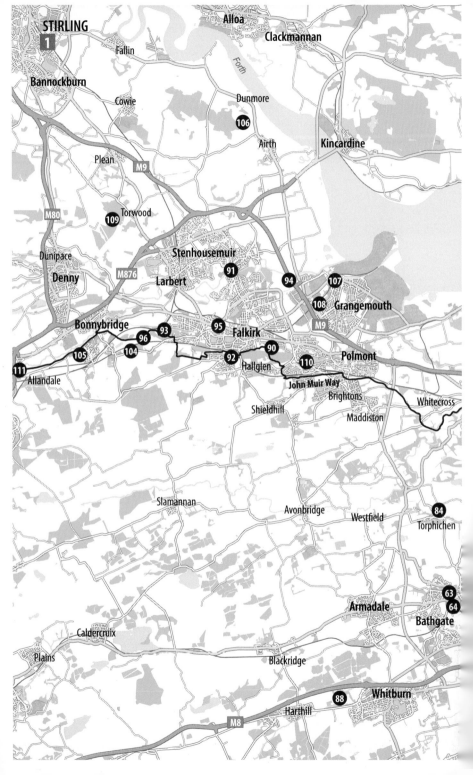

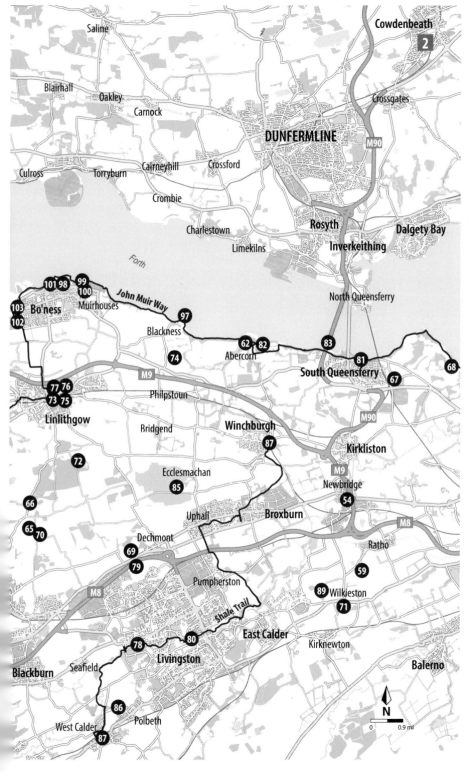

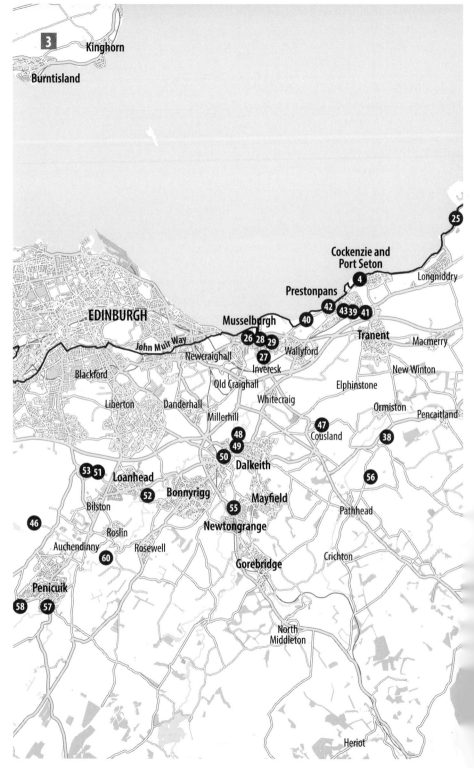

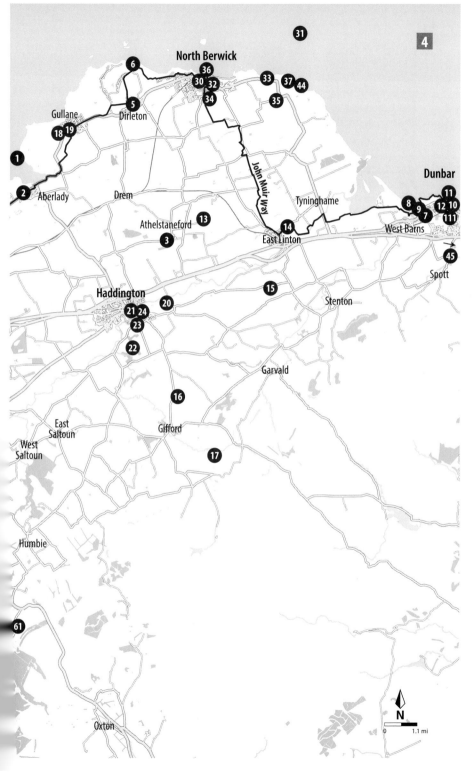

Gillian Tait
111 Places in Edinburgh
That You Shouldn't Miss
ISBN 978-3-7408-1476-2

Tom Shields, Gillian Tait
111 Places in Glasgow
That You Shouldn't Miss
ISBN 978-3-7408-2237-8

Gillian Tait
111 Places in Fife
That You Shouldn't Miss
ISBN 978-3-7408-0597-5

David Taylor
111 Places in the Scottish
Highlands That You
Shouldn't Miss
ISBN 978-3-7408-2064-0

David Taylor
111 Places in Newcastle
That You Shouldn't Miss
ISBN 978-3-7408-1043-6

David Taylor
111 Places along Hadrian's
Wall That You Shouldn't Miss
ISBN 978-3-7408-1425-0

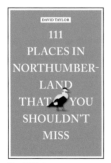

David Taylor
111 Places in Northumberland
That You Shouldn't Miss
ISBN 978-3-7408-1792-3

Ed Glinert, David Taylor
111 Places in Yorkshire
That You Shouldn't Miss
ISBN 978-3-7408-1167-9

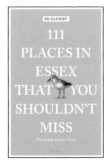

Ed Glinert, Karin Tearle
111 Places in Essex
That You Shouldn't Miss
ISBN 978-3-7408-1593-6

Ed Glinert, David Taylor
111 Places in Oxford
That You Shouldn't Miss
ISBN 978-3-7408-1990-3

John Sykes, Birgit Weber
111 Places in London
That You Shouldn't Miss
ISBN 978-3-7408-2379-5

Alicia Edwards
111 Places for Kids in London
That You Shouldn't Miss
ISBN 978-3-7408-2196-8

Nicola Perry, Daniel Reiter
33 Walks in London
That You Shouldn't Miss
978-3-7408-1955-2

Michael Glover, Benedict Flett
111 Hidden Art Treasures
in London That You Shouldn't
Miss
ISBN 978-3-7408-1576-9

Terry Philpot, Karin Tearle
111 Literary Places in London
That You Shouldn't Miss
ISBN 978-3-7408-1954-5

Jonjo Maudsley, James Riley
111 Places in Windsor
That You Shouldn't Miss
ISBN 978-3-7408-2009-1

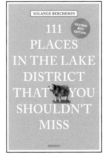

Solange Berchemin
111 Places in the Lake District
That You Shouldn't Miss
ISBN 978-3-7408-2404-4

Catriona Neil, Adrian Spalding
111 Places in Cornwall
That You Shouldn't Miss
ISBN 978-3-7408-1901-9

Acknowledgements

My warm thanks go first of all to Christine Bullick and Clare Mere-
dith, who kindly chauffeured me to the sites in this book that are not
easily accessible by public transport. And a special thank-you to Leo
Stanczyk for coming along to the Scottish Owl Centre.

I would also like to acknowledge the following for their generous
assistance with research and photography during and after my visits
to their places: Ernestine Adriaans (NB Distillery); Ed Bethune and
Gary Donaldson (The Waggonway Project); Alison Bombail (Gosford House); Sean Broadfoot (Cousland Smiddy); Sam and Clover
Christopherson (Coast to Coast Surf School); Julie Cunningham
(formerly of Jupiter Wildlife Centre); Chris Matheson Dear (Linlithgow Union Canal Society); Bill Douglas (Bennie Museum);
Aileen Forbes (Penicuik Papermaking Museum); Lesley Forrest
and Clare Rudyj (Lennoxlove); Tom Fraser (Chippendale School
of Furniture); Will Gibbs, Falkirk Community Trust (Bo'ness Hippodrome); Sally Gouldstone (Seilich Botanicals); Helen Knox and
Ellen Embleton, National Trust for Scotland (House of the Binns);
Svetlana Kukharchuk (The Cheese Lady); John Maule (Amisfield
Walled Garden); Tracy Robertson and Jo Moulin, East Lothian
Museums Service (John Muir's Birthplace); and the stationmaster
and staff of Bo'ness & Kinneil Railway.

In the course of my travels I crossed paths with a number of friendly
fellow rovers who contributed in various ways; I didn't learn all of
their names, unfortunately, but of those I do know I particularly want
to remember Marie and Marty, who guided me to the Ormiston Yew,
and Pete McDougall, for his help at Castlelaw Hill Fort.

I must also mention the key role that cat sitting played in the successful completion of this book, providing me with a series of convenient
bases for visiting sites all across the Lothians and Falkirk District,
as well as the much-appreciated companionship of the following
felines: Louis and Hugo of Prestonpans, Vita and Marta of Musselburgh, Lozzy, Azlan and Pepper of Dunbar, Tilly of Linlithgow,

Bella of Livingston, Mia of North Berwick, Maggie of Allandale, Miss Moneypenny of North Berwick, Harry of Roslin, Vixen of Wallyford and Bonnie and Bartolo of Dalmeny.
Finally, I'd like to express my continuing gratitude to Laura Olk of Emons for her patience and support with what has been an unexpectedly lengthy project.

Gilian Tait was born in Edinburgh and grew up in other parts of Scotland. She studied art history and painting conservation at the universities of Edinburgh and London respectively, and worked in the museum sector for many years before reinventing herself as a writer and photographer. She is the author and photographer of *111 Places in Edinburgh That You Shouldn't Miss* and *111 Places in Fife That You Shouldn't Miss*, and also contributed to *111 Places in Glasgow That You Shouldn't Miss* as photographer and editor. In her spare time she enjoys singing and performing in opera, operetta and musical theatre, and improving her Italian. She has lived in the heart of Edinburgh's Old Town for nearly 40 years.

The information in this book was accurate at the time of publication, but it can change at any time. Please confirm the details for the places you're planning to visit before you head out on your adventures.